SMART MONEY

SMART MONEY

How **HIGH-STAKES FINANCIAL INNOVATION** *is* **RESHAPING OUR WORLD—*for the* BETTER**

ANDREW PALMER

BASIC BOOKS

A Member of the Perseus Books Group

New York

Published by Basic Books,
A Member of the Perseus Books Group

Books published by Basic Books are available at special discounts for bulk purchases in the United States by corporations, institutions, and other organizations. For more information, please contact the Special Markets Department at the Perseus Books Group, 2300 Chestnut Street, Suite 200, Philadelphia, PA 19103, or call (800) 810-4145, ext. 5000, or e-mail special .markets@perseusbooks.com.

Designed by Cynthia Young

Library of Congress Cataloging-in-Publication Data
Palmer, Andrew, 1970–
    Smart money : how high-stakes financial innovation is reshaping our world-
    for the better / Andrew Palmer.
        pages cm
    Includes bibliographical references and index.
    ISBN 978-0-465-06472-4 (hardback) — ISBN 978-0-465-04059-9
(e-book)   1. Banks and banking—Technological innovations.   2. Finance—
Technological innovations.   I. Title.
HG1709.P35 2015
332.1—dc23

                                                    2014041326

10 9 8 7 6 5 4 3 2 1

For Julia, Eliza, Joe, and Kasia

CONTENTS

PREFACE

When I was offered the job of the *Economist*'s banking correspondent in the early summer of 2007, my reaction was one of apprehension. Banking was not an industry that I knew anything about. I had a bank account and a mortgage, knew a couple of friends who had gone into the industry and owned much bigger houses than mine, and that was about it. Grappling with the ins and outs of bond markets and bank balance sheets was not just going to be unfamiliar ground—I assumed that it was also going to be boring as hell.

As far as I was concerned, this was an industry that remorselessly piled up profits. The previous few years had seen an epic expansion of bank returns. The largest one thousand banks in the world reported aggregate pretax profits of almost $800 billion in fiscal year 2007–2008, almost 150 percent higher than in 2000–2001. Banking boasted the largest profit pool in the world in 2006, according to McKinsey, a consulting firm, at 11 percent of the global total.

My professional life was about to consist of interviewing people who made money hand over fist and would presumably continue to do so for as long as I wrote about them. They might be greedy, they might be arrogant, but they certainly knew what they were doing. I didn't realize it at the time, but I was already thinking like a financial regulator.

Fears of a life of tedium turned out to be a bit misplaced. I started on the banking beat in September 2007. The summer had already seen large parts of the financial markets take fright. The downturn in America's subprime-mortgage market had made it impossible for investors to value their holdings of securities backed by these types of loans. The interbank markets, where banks loan money to each other, had suddenly seized up, as institutions realized that they could not be sure of the standing of their counterparties. Something unexpected was happening to the moneymaking machine.

My very first week in the job coincided with a deposit run at Northern Rock, a British lender that came unstuck when it could no longer fund itself in the markets. Some of my earliest interviews on the beat were with people dusting off the manual on how to deal with bank runs. Organizing guide ropes inside bank branches was one tactic: better that than have people spill out onto the street, signaling to others that they should join the line. One HSBC veteran happily recounted stories of the financial crisis that gripped Asia in the late 1990s, when tellers were instructed to bring piles of cash into view to reassure people that banks were overflowing with money.

Tales of improvisation from Asia were not supposed to be relevant to the West's ultrasophisticated financial system. But far worse was to come. A chain of events was under way that would lead in time to the collapse of Lehman Brothers, a huge US investment bank, state takeovers of swaths of the rich world's banking systems, a deep global recession, and the Eurozone debt crisis. I observed these later phases of the crisis from the position of the *Economist*'s finance editor, a post that I held from July 2009 until October 2013.

The crisis would lead to a complete reversal in public attitudes toward the financial industry. The decade leading up to the crisis was one in which finance was lionized. Policy makers applauded the march of new techniques, such as securitization, that appeared to send risk away from the banks and spread it more evenly throughout the financial system. Belief in the efficiency of markets was so pervasive that the skeptics were both few in number and easily dismissed.

The events of the past few years have shattered the belief of outsiders in finance's infallibility. That is an entirely good thing. The system is far less Darwinian than the bankers would like to believe. Banking is not the only industry that gets government handouts—in October 2013 the US government booked a loss on the $50 billion bailout of General Motors, and I don't see much public discussion of the evils of the car industry—but it has clearly benefited from a safety net that others do not have. Nor is it really the law of the jungle for individuals in banking. I have met a lot of very bright people in the financial industry, but I have also met some very mediocre ones, and pretty much all of them seem to remain employable.

But when things go so badly wrong, the pendulum almost inevitably swings too far in the other direction. Another type of consensus has emerged, one in which finance is demonized, in which bankers are generally bad, in which there is a "socially useful" bit of the industry that doles out loans to individuals and businesses, and the rest of it is dangerous, unnecessary gambling. Such anger is understandable. But it also has the effect of distorting the public view of the industry.

CHRIS SHEPARD IS THE kind of person that people have in mind when they lament the pull of finance for society's brightest minds. The youthful American used to wear a lab coat working for Genentech, a biotechnology company whose stated mission is to "develop drugs to address significant unmet medical needs." You don't get much more noble than that. Yet Shepard turned his back on the bench, first for a master of business administration (MBA) and a spell in management consulting and then for the world of high finance. His conversation is peppered with references to equity tranches and bond coupons, balance-sheet volatility and payment triggers.

Shepard founded a venture called Structured Bioequity (SBE). The problem he was trying to address is the harm that can be done to a small biotech firm if one of its drugs fails during clinical trials. Clinical trials are designed to gradually widen the pool of people that a new drug is tested on, and their results are very unpredictable. About 85 percent of therapies fail in early clinical trials. Shepard was particularly focused on the risks involved in Phase II trials, when tests move from a very small group of human guinea pigs to a larger one.[1]

For a very big pharmaceutical firm, with deep pockets and a fatter pipeline of new drugs, a failed trial need not be the end of the road; it can write another check in order to keep development teams together. For smaller firms, which often have no more than two or three drugs in the queue, the damage caused by an unsuccessful clinical trial can be terminal. If the lead drug of one of these firms fails, the entire value of the company can be lost, and it may well fold. The knowledge gained from working on a particular drug scatters, along with the chances of a better outcome the next time around.

Shepard's idea works like an insurance policy. Investors in effect indemnify the firm against a failed clinical trial, promising to pay out an agreed amount in that event so that the firm can rebuild its portfolio. In return, SBE offers the chance for investors to participate in the upside of a successful drug, by turning the amount indemnified into an equity stake in the company upon successful completion of clinical trials. By including enough drugs in the portfolio that is being protected, Shepard thinks that investors can be reasonably confident that some medicines will make it to market. And that in turn should mean that promising medical research is not lost when a particular avenue is closed off.

Progress in getting the first investors to bite was slow, as is typical for an entirely new idea, but when I met him in 2013, Shepard was determined to keep going. Asked why he has turned his back on medical research for finance, he shrugs. "I think I can make more of a difference this way than as a scientist." In the wake of the 2007–2008 crisis, that has become an arresting statement to make.

Two broad misconceptions have taken hold as a result of the convulsions of recent years. The first is that if only finance could turn back the clock, all would be well. Banks never used to run with such low levels of equity funding—the money that shareholders put in and that gets wiped out when banks sustain losses. The securitization markets, where a lot of different income-producing assets such as mortgages get bundled together into a single instrument, never used to be so complex. Stock exchanges never used to be the plaything of algorithms. The temptation is to try to identify a point in financial history when everything worked better and get back to that point. The meme that banking should be boring is widespread. Elizabeth Warren, a Democratic senator from Massachusetts, has used this very phrase to promote a bill that would separate American banks into their comfortingly familiar retail businesses (the ones we all use as customers for checking accounts, mortgages, and the like) and their exotic capital-market businesses (where firms raise money and manage risks).

Yet turning back the clock, as well as being impractical, is no answer. The greatest danger often lurks in the most familiar parts of the financial system. Deposits are seen as a "good" source of funding, even though they can be taken out in an instant and get a giant subsidy in the form of deposit insurance. Property is regarded as a bread-and-butter banking activity but is the cause of banking crisis after banking crisis. Secured lending is seen as prudent, even though it can mean decisions are often made on the basis of the collateral being offered (a house, say) rather than the creditworthiness of the borrower (a borrower with no income and no job, say).

If you look at the write-downs recorded during the crisis, where were they found? In investment banks, yes, but also in the retail and commercial banks. The biggest bank failure in US history was that of Washington Mutual, which collapsed in 2008 with $307 billion in assets and a pile of rotting mortgages on its books. The worst quarterly loss was suffered by Wachovia, another "normal" lender: it chalked up a loss of $23.7 billion in the third quarter of 2008 because of loans kept on its balance sheet. Irish and Spanish banks managed to blow themselves up without the assistance of securitization and credit-default swaps (CDS). The thread running through the financial crisis of 2007–2008 was bad information—about the quality of borrowers, about who had exposure to whom, about how a default in one place would affect other loans—and it brought down every type of institution, simple and complex.[2]

The second misconception concerns the benefits of financial creativity. Few areas of human activity now have a worse image than "financial innovation." The financial crisis of 2007–2008 brought a host of arcane financial processes and products to wider attention. Paul Volcker, one former chairman of the Federal Reserve whose postcrisis reputation remains intact, has implied that no financial innovation of the past twenty-five years matches up to the automatic teller machine in terms of usefulness. Paul Krugman, a Nobel Prize–winning economist-cum-polemicist, has written that it is hard to think of any major recent financial breakthroughs that aided society.[3]

A conference held by the *Economist* in New York in late 2013 debated whether talented graduates should head to Google or Goldman Sachs. Vivek Wadhwa, a serial entrepreneur, spoke up for Google; Robert Shiller, another Nobel Prize–winning economist, argued for Goldman. Wadhwa had the easier task. "Would you rather have your children engineering the financial system creating more problems for us or having a chance of saving the world?" he asked. Even an audience of *Economist* readers in New York was pretty clear about its choice, plumping heavily for Mountain View over Wall Street. Yet Shiller's arguments are the more powerful. "Finance is the place you can make your mark on the world. . . .

You cannot do good for the world by yourself," he told the conference. "Most important activities have to have a financial basis."[4]

This book is divided into two parts. The first is designed to give the reader a broader framework for thinking about financial innovation than just the 2007–2008 crisis and its aftermath. The natural response to the idea of financial ingenuity is to say, "No, thanks." But as the opening chapter demonstrates, the history of human enterprise is also one of financial breakthroughs. The invention of money, the use of derivative contracts, and the creation of stock exchanges were smart responses to fundamental, real-world problems. Financial innovation helped foster trade, smooth risks, create companies, and build infrastructure. The modern world needed finance to come into being.

Without question, the industry did a bad job in the first years of this century of applying itself to big problems. But calling a halt to inventiveness—freezing finance in place, no bright ideas allowed— would not solve the problems associated with the industry. As the second chapter explains, the big risks that finance poses materialize long after the "lightbulb moment." There is a problem with how financial products and markets evolve, but it is a problem that is deeply associated with scale and familiarity, not novelty and creativity.

The third chapter presents a concrete example of how an absence of innovation can be far more damaging than its presence. Property is the world's biggest financial asset and mortgages perhaps the industry's most familiar product. Although people like to think of this as being an area that was taken over by the financial wizards, that is not the right lesson to draw from the crisis. In the United States the industry did come up with inventive ways to pile debt onto inferior borrowers. But in Europe the ordinary mortgage proved just as destructive to many banking systems. Property needs more fresh thinking, not less.

Although there are ingenious people and products in the big institutions, the revolutionary ideas come disproportionately from outsiders. That is common to many industries, not just finance: it takes an unusual firm to blow its own products out of the water; innovation usually comes from new entrants. But the bad habits formed by years of unrestrained profitability seem particularly hard to shake in finance. "When we describe our business, bankers look at us with blank expressions," confides the founder of one financial start-up. "All they can say is: 'But you could be charging more. Why don't you?'"

If the first part of the book makes you doubt that financial innovation is all bad, the second should convince you of its capacity to do good. Despite the crisis—and in some cases because of it—finance is as inventive as it has ever been. The second part looks at some of the efforts being made to resolve an array of enormous social and economic problems.

Many readers of this book will live in countries that need to bring their budgets under control by cutting public spending. Chapter 4 explains how finance can help lure private capital into the gaps left behind. The same readers can also expect to live longer than any generation that has gone before—particularly if people like Chris Shepard can improve drug-development processes. Yet if they are anything like the average citizen, they have far too little saved for their golden years. Chapter 5 looks at some of the industry's initial answers to the downside of longevity.

As dramatically as society is changing, the technological landscape is changing faster still. The Internet is enabling the suppliers and consumers of financing to connect directly rather than via intermediaries. The rise of "big data"—the ability quickly to capture and process huge amounts of information—is improving the way borrowers are screened and risks assessed. At the same time, the crisis has underlined the need for fresh thinking about the way that finance itself operates, so that its worst features (a love of debt, a tendency to forget danger when the going is good) are blunted.

The next four chapters elaborate on both of these themes. Chapter 6 looks at new ways for students to put themselves through school and for new companies to raise early-stage capital. Chapter 7 explores the world of peer-to-peer financing, in which lenders and borrowers bypass the banks altogether. Chapter 8 revisits the world of the subprime borrower to see how the problem of financing the less creditworthy can be solved without blowing up the world economy. Finally, Chapter 9 describes how the old-fashioned virtue of qualitative analysis is being combined with number crunching to mitigate the risk of a new pandemic.

Finance should have been scrutinized more intensively before the crisis. By the same token, it should be looked at with a clear eye now. Bright young people should be going into all sorts of different careers, and finance should be one of them. For all of its flaws, there is no more powerful problem-solving machine.

PART I
LESSONS BADLY LEARNED

CHAPTER 1

HANDMAID TO HISTORY

Financial Sector Thinks It's About Ready to Ruin World Again
  —THE *ONION*

The history of financial innovation is also the story of human advance. The early forms of finance met some very basic needs—trade, safekeeping, credit. As societies and technologies have become more complex, so has finance. When maritime trade became more sophisticated, the banking and insurance industries put down roots. When industrialization created demand for more capital, the era of stock exchanges dawned. When financial instruments became more widely available and finance was democratized, governments responded by creating a more intrusive regulatory framework. When computerization took hold, the age of derivatives—financial products that derive their value from another, underlying, asset—soon followed. For good and bad, the industry that we know today is the product of centuries. And the world that we know today is a product of finance.

Money was the original financial breakthrough. Trade depends on the acceptance of a medium of exchange. Without an agreed form of money—whether notes, precious metals, or cowrie shells—every transaction would involve an arduous negotiation between buyer and seller over what form and quantity of payment would be appropriate. Without money, one of whose properties is that it retains some value over time, anyone who had only perishable goods to barter would find life very tough. You are prepared to accept money as payment because you know you can spend it in the future; you are less happy to accept payment in kiwifruits, say, because they will be exchangeable only for so long as they can be eaten.

Forms of money emerged to grease the wheels of trade as long ago as 9000 BC, when livestock were used as payment. Over time, precious metals emerged as a better form of money: they are less tasty than cows but more portable, durable, and divisible. The first coins were produced in Lydia, in what is now Turkey, in the seventh century BC. The coins were made of electrum, a naturally occurring mixture of gold and silver, and the technology soon spread to Greek cities. The first paper money was invented in China in the ninth century, paving the way for the modern system of fiat money, which is issued by the state and—unlike coins made of precious metals—has no intrinsic value.[1]

Even in modern times, fiat money can still be driven out by commodity forms of exchange. In the immediate aftermath of World War II in Germany, no one had any faith in the Reichsmark, the local currency. Instead, American cigarettes came to be used as the means of payment on the black market: cigarettes were divisible, they lasted well, there was a decent supply of them via imports by American troops, and demand was high—not least because they suppressed appetite in a time of rationing. Money can change its shape to suit the circumstances.[2]

Once ancient societies had an agreed form of exchange that could hold its value, they could develop more ambitious financial instruments. The earliest financial contracts date back to Mesopotamia in the fourth millennium BC: clay tablets inscribed with records of a person's obligation to pay would be sealed inside a type of clay envelope called bullae; these envelopes could themselves act as money, since the obligations they contained were payable to the bearer. Forms of payment ranged from honey to bread, but livestock seems to have been the type of "money" that gave the world the concept of interest. Herds of cattle or flocks of sheep have a natural tendency to multiply: you might lend someone twenty cows, and by the time you get them back, their number will have increased. Those extra heads would have acted as compensation for the risk of lending out the original herd. The evolving language of finance was drawn directly from this pastoral form of interest. The Sumerian word for *interest* was the same as the word for *calves*; the Latin word for *flock* is *pecus*, root of our own term *pecuniary*.[3]

By the time of Hammurabi, a Babylonian king who ruled in the second millennium BC, the role of money and credit had developed to such an extent that the set of laws known as the Code of Hammurabi contained very specific rules on a number of familiar economic relationships. Today we send electronic money into bank accounts for safekeeping; back then, when grain functioned as a means of exchange, the code stipulated terms for grain-storage contracts, an early form of deposit taking. The code also governed relations between debtors and creditors, setting limits on the interest rate that lenders could charge farmers for advancing them equipment, land, and seed and specifying the types of collateral that could be used to secure loans.[4]

In the aftermath of a massive debt bubble, it may seem odd to celebrate the innovation of debt. But it truly is a wonderful invention. Like other forms of finance, debt enables capital to flow from savers to investors (we may not like debt crises, but we also don't much like credit crunches). Lenders are incentivized by the promise of a payback to give money to borrowers; in return, they take on the risk of default. Borrowers give up their claim to some of their future income in return for the capital they need now. Debt's special magic is what economists like to call "intertemporal exchange." People have two forms of capital: they have financial capital, which is the money they actually accumulate, and they have human capital, which is their potential to make money through their future earnings. These two forms of capital are out of sync. Old people have depleted their human capital but have (hopefully) accumulated financial capital. Most young people have a lot of human capital but not much cash. Finance is what bridges the gap between these two states. In the time of Hammurabi, for example, farmers would borrow what they needed to cultivate land in return for payments that would come out of their future income.

It is no different today. The acts of saving and borrowing are both forms of time travel: they are transactions that we undertake with our future selves. We save in order to fund the older us—the retirement from the job we do not yet have or the tuition fees for the children we do not have with the partner we have not met. The more connected we feel to our future selves, the more likely we are to save for "them." Studies indicate that people who are shown a digital avatar of themselves in old age are more likely to put money aside for retirement. Similarly, young people are able to borrow now by unlocking the earnings power of their future selves. When a lender gives you a thirty-year mortgage, it is in effect contracting with the higher-paid, grayer-haired edition of yourself.[5]

Debt is not the only form of financing, of course. Debt entails an obligation to repay, but it also caps the income for lenders to an agreed amount of interest. This obligation on the borrower reduces the risk to creditors, particularly when a loan is secured by collateral (in the way that a house secures a mortgage). But the rewards are correspondingly lower, too: however well a borrower does, the income paid to the lender does not exceed the agreed amount. Equity offers a different proposition to investors. The risks are higher because equity holders get only what's left when the creditors have been paid off; however, the potential rewards are also greater because the owners will share in all the profits if the venture is a success.

Ancient societies also developed various contracts for equity: the Romans had an early form of business corporation called the *societas publicanorum,* which allowed people to buy and sell shares in partnerships that provided outsourced public services. Maritime trade in medieval Italy was fostered by a form of partnership called the *commenda,* in which one partner invested labor and the other put in money; the profits from the journey were split between the two parties, with a common division being 75 percent to the moneyman and 25 percent to the traveler. As well as being a financial contract, the *commenda* also defined the obligations that the traveler had to carry out when he was voyaging. This was an early attempt to solve the "principal-agent" problem that bedevils corporate governance today, in which shareholders have to rely on managers to exercise good judgment in running the companies they own.[6]

Equity and debt enable people with money to spare to allocate it to people who need capital. They are also ways of sharing risk, another of finance's most fundamental jobs. Lenders can spread their money around a lot of different borrowers, as can equity investors, reducing their concentration of risk. By the same token, sharing equity in a company means that the original owners can diversify their risks rather than locking up all their money in one venture.[7]

This same principle of diversification underpins the origins of another vital arm of finance: insurance. Maritime trade again provided much of the initial impetus for a product that offered protection against the worst. Chinese merchants are thought to have self-insured by splitting their cargoes up among several vessels to reduce the chance of a catastrophic loss from any one ship sinking. The Code of Hammurabi contained clauses on "bottomry," a loan secured against the keel, or bottom, of a ship that also functioned as a form of insurance because the loan was forgiven if the vessel sank. The Romans had a very similar arrangement, the *foenus nauticum*, in which an insurer loaned a merchant the funds to undertake a voyage. The debt was canceled if the ship was lost, but returned along with a bonus if the voyage was completed. The basic idea is not that different from the catastrophe (or cat) bonds that we will meet later in the book.[8]

The world's oldest extant insurance contract was struck in Genoa in 1298, with an agreement between a wheeler-dealing merchant named Benedetto Zaccaria and two external investors named Enrico Suppa and Baliano Grillo. In fact, the contract is far more convoluted than a simple insurance arrangement. Zaccaria's fortune was built on importing alum—an all-purpose compound used in everything from dying textiles to making glues—from the Black Sea to western Europe. His contract with Suppa and Grillo centered on the transportation of thirty tonnes of alum to Bruges in modern-day Belgium, which he sold to them for an upfront sum before the cargo had begun its voyage. So far, so simple. But the parties also agreed to an option to repurchase, whereby if the alum arrived safely in Bruges, Zaccaria could buy it back from Suppa and Grillo at a higher price. As for the insurance element of the deal, if the alum was damaged because of a mishap en route, then the two counterparties were liable for the loss in value.[9]

It's all a bit of a blow to those who complain about the complexity of modern finance. The option to repurchase the alum that Zaccaria worked out with his negotiating partners is an early example of a derivative, a financial instrument whose value derives from another, underlying, asset. An option gives the buyer the right, but not the obligation, to buy or sell an underlying asset. An option to buy a share at ten dollars in six months' time, say, is known as a call option; a put option gives the buyer the right to sell the same share at a specified price. Yet options predated even Zaccaria by more than fifteen hundred years. The first known call option was described by Aristotle, who recounts the story of a philosopher named Thales of Miletus (now part of Turkey), who paid a deposit for all the olive-oil presses in Miletus and Chios. This was, in effect, an option to control the market, a bet that paid off handsomely when that year's crop of olives was a good one and Thales was able to charge pretty much what he wanted to have them pressed.

THE HISTORY OF FINANCE until medieval Italy reveals something that can be easily forgotten in the aftermath of the recent global financial crisis: how essential finance is to solving some very basic human requirements. Whether providing a way of storing wealth, of connecting capital with investments, of bridging the gap between the present and the future, or of sharing and managing risk, finance has helped people to meet their objectives since the very earliest civilizations.

But from the start, these new financial instruments posed a problem—working out which people are going to be able to pay back their loans, which enterprises are going to make the most money for their owners, and which risks are likely to materialize. Whether you are a Babylonian lender or a Wall Street banker, these issues get at the essence of finance. The true currency of the industry is information: about the prospects of certain companies, the creditworthiness of borrowers, the probability of different events, and the value of collateral. Information is what brings investors and borrowers together on exchanges and in bilateral contracts, and almost every problem that we will encounter in this book can be resolved into a question of how to gather, assess, and transmit information.

The lending problem is a prime example of the informational challenge: how do you pick the best borrower? There are various ways of solving this problem. One option is for creditors to loan money only to those people they know personally. The friends-and-family approach to finance draws on bonds of trust and familiarity to reduce the risks of default. But it also reduces the amount of lending that goes on. If an economy is to provide capital beyond a certain scale, you need a mechanism that brings together a lot of different lenders and many different borrowers who do not know each other. You need an intermediary that takes the savings of some people and matches that money with creditworthy borrowers. In other words, you need a bank.

There were institutions in ancient Greece and in Rome that we would recognize as forerunners of banks, money changers who provided safe-deposit boxes for people to store their money and then used that money to provide loans. Wealth accrued to bankers from the start: in the fourth century BC, a former slave named Pasion rose to run a large private bank and become one of Athens's richest citizens. By the time of the Roman Empire, funds were being stored, pooled, and reallocated in a manner that we would just about recognize today.

The fall of the Roman Empire paved the way for the Dark Ages, one characteristic of which was a less sophisticated financial system. Banking had to be reinvented all over again in the medieval Italian city-states—places such as Venice, Florence, and Genoa. Financiers would work from benches or counters in the trading halls of these Renaissance cities, financing farmers, insuring buyers against crop failures, and providing a storage place for bills of exchange.

The word *bank* is supposedly derived from *banca*, the Italian word for *counter*; *bankrupt* may be a corruption of *banca rotta*, or *broken counter*.

The invention of the bank was a response to the constraints of relationship-based finance. An intermediary could bridge the gap between lenders and borrowers, providing a place where pools of capital could come together and develop a specialized expertise in assessing the creditworthiness of borrowers. The intermediary could also reap the benefits of diversification: by making a lot of different loans, a bank would reduce the probability that any one of them could scupper the institution if it went bad.

The bank also offered an ingenious solution to another problem: the illiquidity of long-term investments, which required lenders to lock up their money for years until they got it back. The bankers of medieval Italy and the goldsmiths of medieval London soon noticed that when people deposited coins and valuables with them for safekeeping, they didn't all want to have them back at the same time. At any given moment, there was a pile of coins in the vault that were just sitting idle. Why not use them as funding for new loans?

The same logic applies today. Banks do not sit on your deposits, waiting for you to turn up and request your cash back. Because they assume that depositors will not all pull their money out at once, banks loan that money out to people who want to borrow and keep only a fraction of it on hand to meet depositors' demand for cash. That enables banks to pull off two very important tricks. First, by loaning a proportion of all the money they get in as deposits, banks multiply the amount of money in circulation. Second, banks can achieve what the experts like to call "maturity transformation." In English what that means is that banks borrow money at a shorter duration than they loan money out.

The classic example of this maturity transformation is the deposit and the mortgage. Your deposit is a liability for the bank that holds it—it has to be repaid. Unless otherwise specified, it is also instantly redeemable. That means you can get your money out whenever you want: it is the ultimate in short-term lending. A mortgage, by contrast, can last for twenty or thirty years. A short-term debt is transformed into a long-term asset, which makes everyone happy. Creditors don't have to lock their money up for years, borrowers can draw on their long-term future income, and banks can make money in the middle because the rate they pay to borrow money short is less than the rate they can charge to loan money long. Society benefits, too: long-term investments can be financed far more easily because they do not require creditors to sacrifice liquidity.

The downside of maturity transformation is that a lot of creditors do sometimes want their money back at the same time. The most visible manifestation of this is the bank run, with people lining up outside branches to retrieve their cash. A bank run is the moment when the magic of maturity transformation is revealed as a cheap trick. The bank doesn't have deposits on hand to meet demand, so the customers who turn up first are the ones who get their money back. Everyone has an interest in joining the run. The purpose of deposit insurance, which was introduced in the United States in the 1930s and is common to most but not all countries, is to prevent runs by reassuring people that they will never lose money below a certain threshold, even if the bank goes bust.

BANKS SOLVE THE PROBLEM of liquidity by standing in between savers and borrowers, promising the former instant access to their money even as they loan it out for long periods to the latter. Public securities markets take a different approach to liquidity: they provide a place for buyers and sellers to connect directly. That means an owner of a security (either debt or equity) can, in theory, sell it whenever he or she wants to do so.

The first securities markets also date back to medieval Italy, where city-states such as Venice and Genoa forced their well-to-do citizens to loan them money but then consolidated the debt into bonds—instruments that could be sold to others. But the dawn of the era of stock exchanges dates to seventeenth-century Amsterdam, and once again maritime trade was central to the story.

Shipping companies were conventionally financed on an expedition-by-expedition basis: they were liquidated once the voyage had been made. The Dutch East India Company (VOC, to use its Dutch acronym) was founded in 1602 and was granted a twenty-one-year monopoly over Dutch trade with its Asian colonies. The VOC immediately raised capital for expansion in a public offering that entitled its owners to a share of its earnings. That was revolutionary enough, but what really matters for our story is the fact that the directors of the VOC first ignored a ten-year interim deadline for liquidating the company and then later requested an extension of its twenty-one-year charter, which was granted. Investors in other shipping companies ran big risks, but they had previously been confident that a liquidation would return their money to them. The VOC closed that exit door. It had a fixed amount of capital and no intention of winding itself up; it was dissolved only in 1800. To get their money, investors either needed to find a way to live a lot longer or required a secondary market, in which they could sell (and buy) equity when they wanted.[10]

The Amsterdam Stock Exchange fulfilled that role. It rapidly developed many of the attributes of a modern-day exchange. Derivatives quickly emerged. Forward transactions (agreements to buy shares at a fixed price at a future date) started to show up in the documents of Amsterdam notaries a mere five years after the subscription to VOC shares took place in 1602. Options (the right to buy or sell shares at a certain price) and repo transactions (the sale of securities with an agreement to buy them back) soon followed.

Market makers also made their first appearance in Amsterdam. Although markets theoretically allow for buyers and sellers to transact directly, the odds are heavily against a precise match between demand and supply. A seventeenth-century citizen of Amsterdam who wanted to buy some VOC shares might turn up at the newly built exchange building during the designated hour of trading and find an existing shareholder willing to sell in the quantities he wanted. But he also might have to hang around for days on end. The assurance of liquidity came from market makers, intermediaries who held an inventory of VOC shares and cash from which to meet demand from any would-be buyers and sellers.

The first proper market makers seem to have been two seventeenth-century Dutch brothers named Christoffel and Jan Raphoen. The evidence for the Raphoens' role comes from the register of transactions they undertook in VOC shares. Despite making a lot of deals, the capital they kept invested in the company was low on average, which suggests they were making their money by trading in the shares. By providing liquidity, the Raphoens made it easier for people to buy and sell, which in turn made the market more attractive to financial traders and increased the volume of transactions on the exchange. The Raphoens would not recognize the form of their modern counterparts—computerized trading firms that zip in and out of holdings at staggering speeds—but their function would be familiar enough.

THE INSURANCE MARKET also took a big leap forward in the seventeenth century, thanks to the forgetfulness of a London baker named Thomas Farynor. His failure to properly put out the ashes of a fire at his shop on Pudding Lane led to a blaze that started in the early hours of September 2, 1666, and four days later had spread across the center of the city and destroyed 13,200 homes. The Great Fire of London remade London's skyline: the task of rebuilding St. Paul's Cathedral and fifty other churches was handed to Sir Christopher Wren in its aftermath.

The Great Fire also sparked an idea in the mind of Nicholas Barbon (catchy middle name: If-Jesus-Christ-Had-Not-Died-For-Thee-Thou-Hadst-Been-Damned), an energetic and aggressive doctor turned property developer. His Insurance Office is thought to have been the world's first insurance firm and provided fire-insurance protection to London home owners in return for a premium. His was a private-sector response to the vulnerabilities exposed by the Great Fire. Like the rival firms that soon emerged, Barbon's company employed watermen working up and down the Thames to act as private firefighting forces in the event of a blaze. It also used the power of market pricing to start to influence the behavior of home owners, charging far higher premiums for houses made of wood than for those made of brick.[11]

Barbon's venture hit on a very different logic from that of conventional maritime-insurance contracts. Just as shipping companies had had finite life spans until the VOC came along, the first insurance agreements were struck for individual voyages. The likes of Barbon were not interested in underwriting just one house against the risk of fire. Insurance needs to write protection against more risks not only in order to make more money but also to be *safer*. The wonky definition of this "law of large numbers" is that the more exposures an insurer can underwrite, the greater the probability that its actual losses will equal its expected losses.

One way of demonstrating this proposition is to use a device called a Galton Board (see figure 1), which consists of rows of evenly spaced pegs on an upright board. The pegs in each row are staggered, so that when a ball is dropped from the top of the board, it hits a peg in the first row, a peg in the next row, and so on. Each time it hits a peg, the ball has a fifty-fifty chance of going either right or left. But because it will have to take more deviations in a single direction on its way down to end up at the sides, a ball is much more likely to end up in the middle of the board by the time it reaches the bottom. A few might end up at the extremes, but most will end up clustering in the middle in what statisticians call a "normal distribution." If you drop only one ball, you might get unlucky and have one of the oddballs at the edges. But the more balls you drop, the closer your average outcome gets to the expected outcome. Large numbers reduce the odds of an unusual average outcome.

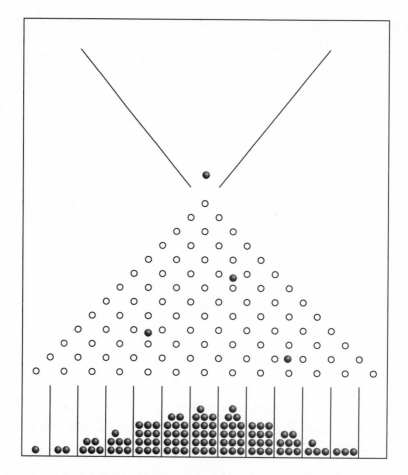

Example of a Galton Board. *Source: Marcin Floryan*

In thinking about the course of financial innovation, mathematical insights like the law of large numbers have a large part to play. This particular idea was formalized by Jacob Bernoulli, a Swiss mathematician, in a posthumous work published in 1713. But the advances made by finance ever since medieval Italy have been pulled along in large part by mathematical breakthroughs.

"Quants," the name given to the mathematical whiz kids who now pervade the industry, were a big part of finance before the term was even coined.

One of the earliest practitioners of financial mathematics was Leonardo of Pisa (1170–1240), who is better known to us as Fibonacci. His *Liber Abaci,* or Book of Calculation (1202), is most famous for outlining the Fibonacci sequence (in which numbers are the sum of the previous two: 1, 1, 2, 3, 5, 8, and so on) that is observable in many natural settings. But it also contains a number of practical calculations that are very familiar to modern finance. One was a technique that allowed merchants to calculate the relative values of spices such as saffron and pepper, just as modern-day arbitrageurs assess the relative values of different securities in the hope of exploiting anomalies in their pricing. Another was a way of dividing profits among the financial investors in a *commenda* when there was more than one of them. Perhaps the most important of Fibonacci's insights was a method for working out the "present value" of cash flows—that is, how much a future amount of money is worth today, given that money can earn interest in the meantime. The process of "discounting" is central to financial analysis today—from businesses working out whether to invest in a new plant to pension schemes assessing whether they have enough money to pay their members' retirement benefits—and is connected to Fibonacci by an eight-hundred-year thread.[12]

If Fibonacci's contribution to finance is little known compared to his more famous observation, the same goes for Edmond Halley. Another of the great polymaths that previous ages routinely turned out, Halley was an English astronomer royal who gave his name to the comet that is visible from earth every seventy-five to seventy-six years (its next visit is due in 2061). The comet won him immortality, but his major financial breakthrough was concerned with death. Halley developed the first proper "life table," which used demographic data from the German city of Breslau to calculate how many people in the city were alive at every age up to eighty-four. His numbers showed that there were, for example, 1,000 people alive aged one, 855 aged two, 798 aged three, and so on. That information then enabled him to calculate the present value of life annuities (an insurance product that pays an income to someone until someone's death) based on the age of the person insured and the likely number of years left to him and on interest rates. If the actuarial profession has a Big Bang moment, Halley's 1693 paper on life annuities is it.[13]

The annuities business also saw the principle of diversification being taken to another level, in an approach that foreshadowed the development of securitization. The essence of securitization is that it smooshes together a lot of different income-generating assets (mortgages, car loans, rental payments, and so forth) into a single security. The concept goes back at least as far as prerevolutionary France. The eighteenth-century French state used to raise money by selling life annuities (*rentes viagères*). A creditor would pay a sum of money upfront, and the state would pay him (or her) an annuity for the remainder of his life. These policies were the major source of new loans after 1750 and the largest component of France's public debt by 1789. Initially, the size of annuities used to vary depending on the age of the buyer: older adults with less time to live on average received higher payments, and younger annuitants received smaller amounts. But from 1770 the French state paid a flat rate no matter what the age of the annuitant.[14]

People may suffer from all sorts of behavioral flaws when it comes to money matters. But they seem to be pretty damned good at exploiting glaring financial opportunities. The change to a single annuity amount meant that an annuity that paid out for a young person was worth more than one for an older person. It was perfectly permissible in those days for people to buy annuities on the lives of third parties, so the obvious thing to do was buy annuities on the lives of children who had gotten through the dangerous years of infancy but were still very young and had many more years of payments ahead of them. The amount of money that the French state was paying out on nominees aged between five and fifteen far exceeded the payments for any other age. The tendency for a product or market to attract higher-risk customers is known as "adverse selection," and on this occasion adverse selection was working to the detriment of the French. The ideal annuitants would have been those with the fewest years left on the planet; instead, the French were committed to doling out money to those with the longest to live.

The ones who moved most aggressively to take advantage of this opportunity were bankers from Geneva. But they had problems to negotiate. Most important, a child could still die young, leaving the buyers of the annuity badly out of pocket. So the Geneva banks, through their branches in Paris, diversified the risk. They began to select young girls from Geneva families, chosen especially for the families' record of longevity and only after surviving smallpox. These girls were then grouped together in pools, the most common denomination being thirty lives, which is why the scheme

became known as the *trente demoiselles de Genève* (thirty maidens of
Geneva). Portions of these annuity pools were then sold on to individual investors, who could take comfort from the banks' selection
processes that they were investing in high-quality assets. An investment in cash flows based on a diversified pool of assets selected
and packaged by bankers? To those who recall the logic behind
the bundling of American mortgages into securitized bonds, it all
sounds faintly familiar.

Finance's early flirtations with the world of "big data"—using a
combination of mathematics and data to speed pricing and manage
risks better—also suffered a familiar failing. Relying on the idea of
normal distribution, in which most outcomes cluster in the middle
of an expected range and only a few sit off at the edges, means that
extreme risks tend to be underplayed. That is what happened in the
recent financial crisis, when the extreme risk of a national house-
price downturn in the United States was ignored. It also tripped
up the Genevans. For them, the extreme risk was not just a disaster or pandemic that would kill their investments. There was also
the problem of "counterparty risk." Even if your girls survived into
old age, the bet would pay off only if the counterparty—that is,
the French state—kept paying up over the course of their entire
lifetimes. That gamble failed. After the French Revolution, the national debt was restructured in 1794, with investors in annuities on
younger lives suffering losses.

FINANCE IS PUSHED forward by multiple propellers. One is the
power of events, such as the Great Fire of London. Another is
progress in assessing information, whether theoretical insights like

Fibonacci's or practical applications like Halley's tables. Another still is the development of new technology. The needs of maritime trade helped push finance forward until the middle part of the second millennium. Another form of transportation—the railways—gave it the next big shove.

Laying mile after mile of railway track was a capital-intensive business: at the peak year of construction in Britain in 1847, the railways absorbed investments worth almost 7 percent of the country's gross domestic product in a single year. (By comparison, the massive telecom boom of the 1990s absorbed capital totaling 1–1.5 percent of America's GDP over a period of several years.) That meant companies had to lay their hands on very large amounts of money. The idea of the joint-stock firm as a means of raising capital from a lot of investors was already in place, thanks to exchanges like that in Amsterdam. Techniques such as calculating net present value gave investors and bankers the theoretical tools to work out which projects to back. But the railways posed all sorts of new challenges.[15]

One challenge related to the informational problem of screening. If the job of finance is to allocate capital to productive ventures, it needs to find a way of distinguishing the good bets from the bad and then monitoring their progress once the money has been deployed. Whereas previous technologies had been restricted in geographical scope, allowing local providers of capital to assess projects fairly easily, the railways spanned great distances and pushed into remote areas, particularly in the United States. Relationship-based finance was again pushing up against its natural limits.

Specialized financial institutions emerged to help channel capital to the railroads and to oversee investments by serving on the boards of railway companies they backed. And as the railways turned more and more to securities markets to raise money, they spawned new forms of standardized information to help far-flung investors make their decisions. Credit-reporting firms appeared: the firms that would eventually merge to become Dun and Bradstreet were born during the middle of the nineteenth century. A trade press sprang up to cover the industry. Between 1849 and 1862, the editor of the *American Railroad Journal* was one Henry Varnum Poor, whose firm would later be the Poor in Standard & Poor's (S&P). As the railroad boom continued and the demand for transparent information grew, it fell not to Poor but to another famous industry name, John Moody, to produce the first credit ratings, in 1909. The first ratings that he produced were all on the debts of US railroad companies. Along with Standard & Poor's and Fitch, Moody's remains one of the industry's big three names.[16]

Mention of credit ratings reminds us that finance does not always succeed in its task of assessing risks. When investors get excited by a new technology, careful screening easily gives way to desperate scramble. The history of the industry is also a history of greed, speculative excess, get-rich-quick dreams, and get-poor-quicker investments—peppered here and there with fraud and deceit. To see how little things have changed over the years, pick up a copy of a tract called *Confusion de Confusiónes,* written by a Sephardic Jew from Portugal named Joseph de la Vega and first published in 1688. De la Vega's subject is the Amsterdam Stock Exchange, and in it he paints not only a landscape of familiar products but also a gallery of familiar behaviors. He observes "herding," in which investors copy the behavior of others; overconfidence; overtrading, which still ends up costing investors today because of the excessive transaction costs they incur; and the "disposition effect," in which people hold on to losing investments for far too long.

That's just in normal times. Occasionally, people really lose their heads. In the 2000s, the mania was for property; in the 1990s, it was for dot-com companies; in the mid-nineteenth century, it was for railways. Britain's 1840s railway boom turned into a speculative bubble that ended up hitting the wallets of affluent investors, including Charles Darwin, John Stuart Mill, and the Brontë sisters. In 1855 the *Economist* wrote that "the railways, with all their multiplied conveniences and contrivances, are an honour to our age and country: commercially, they are great failures."[17]

Financial distress is another spur to innovation, however. When US railroads got into trouble en masse at the back end of the nineteenth century, many confronted the downside of debt: it entails a relentless obligation to repay, no matter what the circumstances. As railroad companies sought to find ways to reduce the burden of fixed repayments, new financial instruments emerged: preferred shares, which gave their owners priority over ordinary shareholders in terms of dividend income but also handed management the discretion to withhold those payments, were one solution. Income bonds that made debt repayments contingent on profitability were another. Such tinkering enabled railroad companies to sustain high levels of capital expenditure and long payback periods without being tipped into bankruptcy.[18]

Indeed, another way of thinking about the modern history of financial inventiveness is as a series of iterations on the two basic forms of capital—debt and equity. Tinkering with the terms of securities creates instruments that more precisely match the needs of investors and issuers. The examples of preferred stock and income bonds show how capital structures can be refined and cash flows can be made contingent on other events. The first inflation-protected bonds, which safeguard investors' returns against rising prices, were issued by the Commonwealth of Massachusetts in 1780 during the Revolutionary War, as a type of deferred compensation designed to protect American soldiers from the effects of severe price rises. The bonds did so by specifying their value in terms of their purchasing power: "Both Principal and Interest to be paid in the then current Money of said STATE, in a greater or less SUM, according as Five Bushels of CORN, Sixty-eight Pounds and four-seventh Parts of a Pound of BEEF, Ten Pounds of SHEEPS WOOL, and Sixteen Pounds of SOLE LEATHER shall then cost, more or less than One Hundred and Thirty Pounds current money, at the then current Prices of said ARTICLES."[19]

The majority of new products that stream out of finance today are also refinements to existing securities. Often these "new" products are no more than tweaks. Ask a banker what he's proudest of in his career, and the chances are he'll go misty-eyed recalling an arcane first—a new kind of "step-up coupon" on an asset-backed security in Paraguay or something equally obscure.[20]

BY THE TIME OF THE RAILROAD revolution in the nineteenth century, finance had evolved to the point where it could support large-scale industrial enterprises. It was also drawing in more and more people, as wealth and political power became more diffuse. This process of democratization took different forms in different societies. In Japan, for example, finance was an important part of the changing political economy. In modern financial markets, the term *samurai bond* means a bond denominated in yen and issued in Japan by a non-Japanese firm; the first such samurai bond was issued in 1970 by the Asian Development Bank. But there was a forerunner. Of all the groups likely to lose out from Japan's modernization during the Meiji period, the samurai warrior caste had the most at stake. General conscription was introduced in Japan in 1873, eliminating the exclusive right of the samurai to hold military positions. The Satsuma Rebellion of 1877 was the most serious manifestation of samurai discontent: twenty thousand former samurai lost their lives, along with six thousand government troops.

That defeat played its part in subduing the samurai, but according to Saumitra Jha of Stanford University, finance won them around to the new order. The samurai had traditionally been paid in rice. In 1876 the new central government converted these payments into interest-bearing government bonds: more than three hundred thousand former samurai received the bonds. Bank regulations were changed at the same time, so that banks had to own large amounts of these "samurai bonds," which were exchanged for equity. As a result, by 1882 samurai owned fully three-quarters of the stock of Japan's banks. Owning banks radically reduced the attractiveness of military revolt. The prospect of financial rewards—what Jha terms "the use of financial claims on a shared future"—gave the samurai a stake in Japan's modernization.[21]

In different ways the financial franchise was also being extended in Europe and the United States. Industrialization created a new working class. Savings banks spread across Europe in the nineteenth century as a way of encouraging the poor to put money aside for old age and sickness. And as societies became more prosperous, populations could aim higher than precautionary savings. Investments that had been the preserve of the wealthy started to democratize. America's entry into World War I in 1917, for example, meant that the US government had to issue loads of debt on capital markets; in order to do so, it mounted a nationwide marketing campaign aimed at persuading individuals to buy smaller denominations of debt. By the time the United States issued its "Victory Loan" in 1919, retail investors had discovered an appetite for government debt: 4 million of them subscribed.[22]

The equity markets followed a similar path, from the wealthy investors to the little guy. Charles Merrill first set up a brokerage business called Merrill Lynch in 1915, but it was only in the firm's second coming, during the 1940s, that he explicitly targeted the retail investor. Branches were opened across the United States. Marketing and promotion formed a big part of his strategy. One of the most famous advertisements in American history was a 1948 Merrill Lynch ad in the *New York Times*, a dense six-thousand-word guide to investing called "What Everybody Ought to Know About This Stock and Bond Business." Despite its forbidding appearance, the ad was accessibly written and a huge success: across the years it ran, the firm received more than 3 million responses from retail investors grateful for some simple language about a complex subject. As the century progressed, increasing wealth enabled more and more people to buy their own homes by taking on debt: the home-ownership rate among US households rose from 43.6 percent in 1940 to 64 percent in 1980.[23]

THIS RAPID TOUR THROUGH the history of financial innovation has one last stop: the age of derivatives. Derivatives are financial instruments whose value is derived from the performance of another, underlying, asset. We have seen that derivative instruments have existed for many centuries, from Thales's bet on the olive-oil harvest to the forwards on the price of VOC shares. The world's first futures market traded in rice futures in Dojima in eighteenth-century Japan. But derivatives really took off in the 1970s and 1980s, as new instruments were created to manage the risk of interest rates moving up and down, currencies fluctuating, borrowers defaulting, and commodity prices zipping around.

The first interest-rate future was launched in October 1975. This is an agreement to buy or sell a debt instrument at a specified price at a specified future date. Because the value of a bond rises and falls in an inverse relationship to the trajectory of interest rates, investors who have bought a bond can protect themselves from an interest-rate rise by selling a future: as they lose money on one, they gain on the other. The first futures were for a type of mortgage-backed security; they paved the way for much more actively traded contracts in Treasury-bond futures.

Other types of derivatives followed. The first interest-rate swap, in which a borrower paying a floating-rate loan agrees to swap payments with a borrower who has taken out a fixed-rate loan, was agreed to in 1981. Equity-derivatives contracts based on the S&P 500 index were introduced in 1982. Credit-default swaps, which act as a kind of insurance policy against default by a corporate borrower, were invented in the 1990s. The size of the derivatives markets grew relentlessly in the years leading up to the 2007–2008 crisis, expanding by an annual average rate of 24 percent between 1995 and 2007, much quicker than the equity (11 percent growth) and bond (9 percent) markets.[24]

All of the strands of financial development that were at work in prior centuries were at work during the age of derivatives. First, and inconveniently for finance bashers, genuine needs were being met. The changes to the world's financial system over the past few decades created new risks for banks, companies, and investors to deal with. The end of the Bretton Woods system of fixed exchange rates in the 1970s meant that currencies could rise and fall: foreign-exchange derivatives offered a way to hedge that risk. Big jumps in US interest rates in the early 1980s, as then Federal Reserve chairman Paul Volcker battled inflation, gave people more reason to hedge against interest-rate volatility. Globalization increased the complexity of multinational companies' operations, and the Asian debt crisis in the late 1990s drove home the risks of operating in emerging markets. Credit-default swaps promised a way for banks to reduce the impact of defaults, in the aftermath of a wave of bank failures experienced during America's savings-and-loan crisis in the 1980s, because the sellers of a swap promised a payout if the borrower in question was unable to pay.

Needs are not always so noble, of course. By making their lending seem less risky, credit-default swaps also meant that regulators were happy to allow banks to fund themselves with less equity capital. That in turn made banks more attractive propositions to equity investors, who would have to put up less money in order to get a return. Speculators also came to play in derivatives markets, investing in order to profit from price movements rather than to hedge real risks.

The second impetus behind the derivatives explosion came from another theoretical breakthrough. Options pricing had always been a bit finger-in-the-wind before: there was no good way to put a value on the right to buy or sell something in the future. In 1973 a trio of American academics—Fischer Black, Myron Scholes, and Robert Merton—cracked the problem of what to pay for an option. The answer they came up with, expressed as what is now known as the Black-Scholes equation, was based on a simple idea: two things that had identical outcomes ought to cost the same. The price of the option ought to be the same as whatever it cost to construct an investment portfolio that achieved the same end. The Black-Scholes formula enabled the rapid pricing of options and paved the way for explosive growth in derivatives markets. Greek academics have even used it to work out what Thales should have paid for his olive-oil option more than fifteen hundred years ago.[25]

The third driver was technology. We have seen how a new technology like the railways required finance to adapt in order to provide appropriate financing and screening mechanisms. But new technology can also affect finance more directly, and the computerization of the industry is the prime example. The automation of routine tasks made it more economic for fund managers to manage people's savings, for example, which helped spur the rise of big pools of institutional capital. Institutional investors—professional fund managers like Fidelity or BlackRock—did not exceed 28 percent of total trading volume on the New York Stock Exchange (NYSE) until 1963; by 1969, in parallel with the spread of computing, they accounted for 52 percent of turnover.[26] Advances in technology also turned the Black-Scholes equation from a theoretical advance into a practical one: calculators made by the likes of Texas Instruments and Hewlett-Packard swiftly incorporated the formula, enabling traders to apply the algebra on the exchange floor.

WHAT LESSONS CAN we take from this brief tour d'horizon of financial breakthroughs? One is that those who think the recent global crisis meant the end of history are dead wrong. The big drivers of financial innovation—needs, theoretical insights, and technology—are still powering the industry. Indeed, as we shall see in the second part, they are providing greater momentum than ever before. The ability of the state to raise and spend ever more money is approaching its limit, meaning that the need to bring private capital to bear on problems such as pension provision and welfare spending is more pressing now than it has been since the early part of the twentieth century. The great crisis of 2007–2008 has provided new insights into the behavior of the financial system, ones that many entrepreneurs are seeking to exploit. And the Internet is only now really disrupting the financial industry, offering a third way to join together suppliers and recipients of capital after the invention of banks and institutions and the spawning of exchanges.

Added to that is the impetus given to innovation by new regulations, of which there have been a bucketload since 2008. Again, this is nothing new. The Eurobond market, the first modern international capital market, was turbocharged by a tax imposed by President John Kennedy designed to discourage Americans from investing in foreign securities; international firms turned to the nascent European market for dollar-denominated borrowing instead. Going further back, the "tulipmania" that infected seventeenth-century Dutch buyers, sending the price of tulip bulbs spiraling beyond the cost of a town house in Amsterdam, is usually put down to speculative irrationality. But the very steep increase in prices in early 1637 came about when the government ratified a change in contracts that meant tulip buyers were no longer obliged to buy tulips at an agreed price in the future. This change was the equivalent of altering a futures contract into an options contract and gave investors a much greater incentive to load up on tulips, knowing that they could pay a small fee to cancel the contract if prices did not rise high enough to make it worthwhile exercising the option. Prices soared as a result. In the words of one scholar, the tulipmania was little more than a "contractual artifact." The current burst of regulatory activity is bound to have similar unanticipated effects on how money moves around the financial system.[27]

The idea of another era of financial wizardry is unlikely to thrill many people. The understandable concern is that the last bout of innovation—all those credit-default swaps and complex securitized mortgages—ended pretty badly. But taking the longer view of financial history tells a different story. When societies confront big problems, finance tends to be involved in the solution. As soon as humans started to trade, they needed a means of exchange, or money. As soon as farmers needed capital to buy more animals, they invented credit. As soon as traders made voyages at sea, they wanted insurance to protect them against the risk of shipwreck.

What was true of the ancient world is also true of the modern world. The academic and empirical evidence suggests that financial development and economic growth go together. Comparative studies of Brazil and Mexico between 1830 and 1930 show that Brazil's more aggressive financial liberalization loosened firms' access to external sources of capital and delivered faster industrial expansion than in Mexico. A 2002 analysis of Italy showed that an individual's odds of starting a business increased by a third if he moved from the least financially developed region in the country to the most developed. Cross-country comparisons suggest that financial development reduces income inequality. A study of households in Tanzania showed that a temporary shock to living standards through a loss of crops leads many families to put children to work to mitigate the hit to their income—but families who have access to credit are better able to avoid pulling their kids out of school.[28]

The industry's critics have a ready response to this argument: finance may well be useful but only up to a certain point. There is a moment at which there are diminishing returns to financial development. If the financial industry gets too big, it starts to draw talent away from other sectors. If debt levels go beyond a certain point, the chances of a crisis rise. If the home-ownership rate keeps going higher and higher, then people who don't have the income to sustain a mortgage must eventually be the ones entering the property-owning class. We have seen the disadvantages of such excessive "financialization" most clearly in recent years, such skeptics say, most obviously in the financial crisis of 2007–2008 but also in other areas, such as the automation of the stock exchanges. But this criticism does not strengthen the argument against innovation. If anything, it weakens it, because it underlines that the real problem with finance lies not on the front line of innovation but in the journey that products take from idea to established market.

Chapter 2

FROM BREAKTHROUGH TO MELTDOWN

The previous chapter described how breakthroughs in finance have helped to propel enterprise and realize ambitions throughout human history. But anyone who seeks to defend the industry must also recognize how often, and how badly, it goes wrong. In *This Time Is Different*, their excellent survey of debt crises across the centuries, Carmen Reinhart and Kenneth Rogoff analyze episodes of banking crises. Such meltdowns are depressingly common in both developed and emerging economies: Britain, America, and France have experienced twelve, thirteen, and fifteen episodes of banking crisis, respectively, since 1800, for example.[1]

The first bailout in the United States happened way back in 1792, when a bubble and then a slump in the price of the country's federal debt helped spark widespread panic. Alexander Hamilton, America's first treasury secretary, was desperate to prevent severe damage to the country's nascent financial system. He responded by, among other things, buying up government debt in order to prop up its price and protect the banks that owned it and by channeling cash to lenders that needed it. For the first time in US history, but not the last, the state stepped in when finance got into trouble.

Other countries had already been through booms and busts of their own. In Britain there was the South Sea bubble of 1720, a crash in the share price of the South Sea Company, which had been granted a monopoly to trade with South America. That same year, French investors were hit by the collapse of the so-called Mississippi scheme, under which they subscribed to the shares of a company set up to exploit economic opportunities in what is now the United States. Before that there was the seventeenth-century "tulipmania" in Holland. The ancient world also had its share of financial panics. The Roman Empire endured a crisis in AD 33, when the enforcement of orders requiring that a certain proportion of money be invested at home prompted lenders to call in loans elsewhere, causing widespread financial distress. Finance may propel us forward, but it is also liable to cause a lot of trouble.[2]

This book's contention is that financial innovation is an essential component of attempts to address the world's big problems. How can that argument be squared with the industry's destructive tendencies? The answer lies in the difference between innovation and institutionalization, between the creative spark and the establishment of a proper market. Beyond a certain scale and beyond a certain point in their development, good ideas have a tendency to run wild.

A few financial products are stinkers from the outset, of course. Some of the mortgage products—the negative-amortization mortgage, anyone?—that sprouted at the height of America's recent housing bubble resemble cartoon crates of TNT with an extralong fuse. The end of the structured investment vehicle (SIV), an off-balance-sheet instrument invented to take advantage of loopholes in bank regulations, is not much lamented. The motives behind new products are not always spotless. I remember being with a very senior Lehman banker in London just a few weeks before his employer went bankrupt in September 2008. As we were discussing the latest restrictions imposed against short-selling the shares in banks, a measure designed to protect his own industry, he jerked his head across Canary Wharf in the direction of the regulator's office. "Whatever rule those fucking idiots come up with on Monday, I'll have found a thousand ways around it by Friday," he said. (Not if you've gone bankrupt, you won't.)

But even now it is hard to find fault with the concept, as opposed to the practical application, of many of the most demonized products of the recent past. Take securitization and credit-default swaps. It would be blinkered to argue they have no problems. By handing risks on to someone else, securitization gives banks an incentive to loosen their underwriting standards; they won't be the ones picking up the pieces. The protection afforded by credit-default swaps may similarly blunt the incentives for lenders to be careful when they extend credit, because they will get a payout in the event of a borrower defaulting. But the downsides should not obscure the good. India, with a far more conservative financial system than America's, allowed its first CDS deals to be done after the 2007–2008 crisis, recognizing that the instrument would help attract creditors and build its domestic bond market.

Securitization—which has been around in one form or another since the Geneva bankers were investing in prerevolutionary French debt—means that lending can be done by a greater pool of capital than the banks. European policy makers, primed after the crisis to regard US finance as the source of all evil, are now keen to encourage securitization rather than rely too much on the banking system.

The problem with financial innovation is not that products have original sin, but that the financial system is programmed to change these products in ways that make them more dangerous. More than any other industry, finance evolves through rapid, constant experimentation. The physical constraints on the flow of new products are light. The raw materials of financial innovation are cheap: a fertile mind and a piece of paper will often suffice to dream up new ideas.

Demand for fresh ideas has always been extremely high in finance. The early history of the Amsterdam Stock Exchange is a case in point. Soon after trading started in the shares of the Dutch East India Company in 1602, people quickly began to use them as collateral for borrowing. The very first recorded use of shares for this purpose came in August 1607, when a Dutch nobleman used VOC securities to borrow from a local merchant. By the 1640s, a fully fledged market for this sort of borrowing was up and running, facilitated by the use of standard printed transaction forms. Derivatives markets based on the underlying shares also emerged quickly. Forward contracts—obligations to buy a share at a fixed price at a certain date in the future—began to appear in notaries' records in 1607, as investors speculated on where share prices would head.[3]

It is no different today. A 1989 paper calculated that of all public securities offerings in 1987, almost 20 percent consisted of financial instruments that had not been in existence in 1974. A follow-up paper in 2002 totted up 1,836 unique security codes for new types of public securities offerings from the early 1980s to 2001. And that is to say nothing of the private transactions.[4]

For a new financial instrument to really take off, however, what is needed is a critical mass of users. A lot of users provide the elixir of "liquidity," which captures the idea that someone who owns an asset can quickly sell it and convert it into cash. Liquidity means that the costs of trading securities are reduced, because both buyers and sellers do not have to spend too much time searching each other out. It also stimulates demand by reassuring investors that they will not be stuck in their positions even if they want to sell.

If finance has to find a way for a lot of people to coalesce quickly, it has to standardize. Standardization is what gives buyers and sellers the ability to transact efficiently in markets. If no deal ever got negotiated from scratch, there would never be genuine innovation. If every deal needed to be negotiated from scratch, nothing would ever acquire genuine scale.

This need to agree on common terms has greased the wheels of finance from the start. The world's first futures market, which traded in rice futures in Dojima in eighteenth-century Japan, had standardized contracts specifying which types of rice would be traded for which maturities. It had a clearinghouse that registered transactions, netted out trades to simplify payments, and asked traders to refill their accounts if they had suffered losses. The balance of those accounts was measured using official end-of-day prices that were set by burning a fuse that was attached to a wooden box. As long as the box was on fire, trading could continue. When the fire was burned out, the price at that moment became the official opening price for the next day. Because trading often kept going beyond this point, "watermen" would dash whole buckets of water over the crowd in order to disperse them. The price that prevailed then—the *okenedan,* or "bucket price"—was the settlement price for the day. There were rules for everything.[5]

The need to standardize can be discerned in market after market. Indexes are one example. An index fund spreads risks across a lot of different securities in a fixed and transparent manner by mimicking the constituents of the index in question. The oldest US stock-market index is the Dow Jones Transportation Average, started in 1894; the still-celebrated Dow Jones Industrial Average began two years later; the S&P 500 index, widely considered the best representation of the health of the American stock market, kicked off in 1957.

Derivative deals provide another example. Prior to the founding of the International Swaps and Derivatives Association in 1985, every time a private "over-the-counter" (OTC) swap deal was done, you needed to draw up a thirty-page agreement. ISDA—whose members include banks, asset managers, and companies—helped develop something called the "ISDA master agreement," a set of standard terms that apply automatically to over-the-counter derivatives transactions. ISDA is where banks go when new areas of OTC activity reach a critical mass and custom-made documents no longer do the job. It also acts as Solomon when ambiguities arise: ISDA's determinations committee meets to decide on when credit-default swaps have been triggered, for example.

The London Interbank Offered Rate also has its roots in a search for standardized efficiency. LIBOR is an interest rate that has become central to pricing loans and derivatives worldwide and that we now know was being routinely manipulated before and during the 2007–2008 financial crisis. It is very common to hear a phrase like "the loan was priced at LIBOR plus 60" when you talk to bankers: that means the loan carried an interest rate of whatever LIBOR was, plus another 60 basis points (100ths of a percentage point) on top. So if LIBOR was 5 percent, then the loan would be 5.6 percent.

LIBOR was the brainchild of Minos Zombanakis, a Greek banker working in London in the late 1960s, who was trying to create a market for syndicated loans, in which loans are split between a number of banks. Because these loans were short term and rolled over regularly, the price also changed regularly. Rather than renegotiating terms each time, Zombanakis devised a formula whereby banks within the syndicate would report their cost of funds, and a weighted average of this cost, plus a bit extra for profit, would be the price of the loan until the next period began. This method of averaging the funding costs of a panel of banks eventually morphed into the LIBOR benchmark we know today.[6]

STANDARDIZATION REDUCES frictions, but it also creates problems—and not just because a bigger market can cause more damage when it runs into trouble. It means that less specialized investors can easily join in the fun. And it means that markets can snowball in size, overwhelming the infrastructure built to sustain them and making it more likely that the state will have to step in when things go wrong. "I don't think we should celebrate speedy growth in new areas," says one of the most senior figures on Wall Street. "Growth on a rapid scale means either a brilliant discovery or a mistake: history suggests it is likely to be a mistake."

One of the most thought-provoking academic papers to come out of the 2007–2008 financial crisis is a study by Nicola Gennaioli of Pompeu Fabra University, Andrei Shleifer of Harvard University, and Robert Vishny of the University of Chicago, called "Neglected Risks, Financial Innovation and Financial Fragility." It suffers the usual curses of the economic paper: a crushingly formulaic structure and an enormous amount of algebra. In its very broad outlines, it describes a process of financial euphoria leading to fragility and then crisis that is familiar from the works of economists like Hyman Minsky. Minsky was an American economist who described a process of growing confidence that leads people to take on more and more debt, until the only way it can be safely financed is if asset prices keep rising. At this point, it takes only a small shift in circumstances or attitudes for confidence to evaporate, investors to default, and fire sales of assets to start. That rapid crumbling of confidence is known as a Minsky moment. But the paper's emphasis on the role of safety in explaining financial instability is what resonates most after the events of the past few years.[7]

The authors contend that episodes of financial creativity begin when investors want more of a certain type of product than the market can currently supply. In theory this product could be risky, but in practice demand tends to be greatest for products that are perceived to be safe but also add a little pop to returns. An annual survey by McKinsey & Company of the world's capital markets shows that in 2012, the value of global financial assets (excluding derivatives and physical assets such as property) stood at $225 trillion, $50 trillion of which were "riskier" equities and $175 trillion of which were "safer" loans and bonds.[8]

The precrisis development of America's mortgage market conformed to this model: securitizing mortgages and tranching them created a supply of debt instruments that appeared to be as safe as the limited amount of US Treasuries and managed to deliver a little bit more income than normal government debt. So too did the money-market fund, a financial instrument that offered investors the money-like properties of a bank deposit—in other words, the ability to get your cash back immediately without any loss of principal—but managed to deliver higher income. It is not the dash for risk that lands the world's financial system in trouble; it is the hunt for safe returns.

These new instruments are attended by risks that are different from those of the old ones they are substituting for, however. Putting money into AAA-rated Treasuries is a transparent bet on the full faith and credit of the US government. Putting money into highly rated "collateralized-debt obligations" (CDOs), which bundle up the lower tranches of existing securitizations, was an opaque bet that America would not suffer a national housing-market meltdown. Similarly, putting your money into a bank account is a decision that is informed by an explicit system of deposit insurance: you will get your money back because the government guarantees it. For many, investing in a money-market fund is also a bet on a promise, but this time by a private actor not to "break the buck"— in other words, to give a dollar back for each dollar invested.

These new products may look like the old ones, in other words, but there are differences that investors do not fully appreciate. As a result, when those underappreciated risks do surface, they come as a shock to market participants and prompt panic. Finance can survive many things, but panic is not one of them. The industry has been made more fragile by creating what Gennaioli, Shleifer, and Vishny term *false substitutes*—securities that investors believe to be riskless that turn out to be risky. As bad as things got during the worst of the financial crisis, for example, bank customers remained generally calm. There were runs at a few troubled institutions, but often they were the self-policed kind, as large depositors reduced their balances below the limit for federal deposit insurance. Money-market fund investors were altogether more skittish. A day after Lehman Brothers went bust, the Reserve Primary Fund, the oldest money-market fund, broke the buck when it wrote off its holdings of Lehman debt. Some $300 billion fled the funds in the days following Lehman's bankruptcy, as investors suddenly realized that they were less protected than they had thought. Talk to regulators about the events of September 2008, and they will tell you that nothing was more alarming than this stampede. The only way to stanch the flow was for America's Treasury to issue a temporary guarantee of money-market assets—in effect, to make good on investors' assumptions of safety.[9]

Now if people had peered closely enough at the underlying assets, they would have been less calm. And if investors had been more jittery, the securities could not have substituted for genuinely safe ones. That sort of vigilance is routine when a product is new and niche investors are developing expertise in a market. But as markets develop, the nature of its participants changes.

The diffusion of innovations follows a pattern known as the "S-curve," in which an initial period of early adoption gives way to a period of takeoff and rapid growth, which in turn eventually leads to saturation and a slowing of growth. The S-curve has been observed in the spread of all sorts of products, from cars to televisions. But whereas it doesn't particularly matter to the way the Web works when the technophobes take to the Internet, there is a problem when a great weight of money starts to move into financial markets: prices start to move upward, risk begins to be underpriced, the specialist buyer gets replaced by the generalist buyer. During the most recent crisis, for example, the turning point for one structured-finance veteran in Europe came in the mid-2000s, when he went to the annual securitization-industry conference in Barcelona and it was full of people he had never seen before. "I remember meeting a couple of Icelandic women who said they had £5 million of an ABS deal and that they needed to try and understand it. Securitization was no longer for people who knew what they were doing."

Specialists rely on their own expertise and vigilance to assess risks. Generalists have to use crutches. To help investors like these decipher the contents of each pool of assets during the mortgage boom, some handy rules of thumb—another form of standardization—evolved. Heuristics are very useful, but they can also lead people astray by introducing systematic biases. Such biases are not limited to finance.

One lovely example of how people use rules of thumb comes from a 2011 paper on the used-car market, where researchers wanted to examine the effect of "left-digit" bias.[10] Left-digit bias refers to the human tendency to focus on the left-most number in a string of numbers and to pay less attention to the other digits, which is why this book has far more chance of being priced at $19.99 than $20.00. The researchers analyzed 22 million used-car purchases at wholesale auctions and found that there were very clear jumps in price at each 10,000-mile mark on the car's odometer. Cars with odometer values between 79,900 and 79,999 miles were sold on average for approximately $210 more than cars that had clocked up between 80,000 and 80,100 miles, but for only $10 less than cars with values between 79,800 and 79,899. Sellers respond to these illogical discontinuities by bringing cars to market before the left-most number changes: the researchers found large spikes in the number of cars being auctioned just before each 10,000-mile threshold. Even though the buyers at these auctions are car dealers, it is the buying behavior of the ultimate retail customer that explains the price jumps. The authors estimate that the difference between observed selling prices and the prices that you might expect if every digit on the odometer had been given proper weight adds up to approximately $2.4 billion worth of mispricing.

The example sounds cute, but it matters: first, because buying a car is not a trivial financial decision, so if heuristics are governing behavior in this market, it is reasonable to assume they are doing so in others; second, because the other digits on an odometer are visible but still don't seem to matter. A flawed heuristic is triumphant even in a transparent market.

Being able to override heuristics appears to be a trait of the stars of the financial industry. Financial traders do significantly better than other bank employees in classic tests of cognitive reasoning like the following question: "A bat and a ball cost $1.10 in total. The bat costs $1.00 more than the ball. How many cents does the ball cost?" It may well be that the best traders are those who can switch off the rules of thumb and use a more reflective style of thinking—what Daniel Kahneman, a pioneer of behavioral finance, would call using a System 2 process rather than a System 1 process.[11]

The most recent crisis showed how thin on the ground such stars are. Most investors used fallible heuristics to guide their decision making. Most obviously, home buyers and lenders fell for the rule of thumb that stated house prices in the United States do not fall nationwide. But other heuristics were hard-coded into the financial system by the logic of standardization.

In the world of mortgage securitization, another anchor was the FICO credit score. The FICO score counts as an early example of big data, the crunching of numbers to aid business decision making. The score was the creation of an engineer named Bill Fair and a mathematician named Earl Isaac and first appeared in the late 1950s. Since then the score has become a ubiquitous measure of creditworthiness in the United States, a single-figure distillation of a person's payment and credit history that summarizes his or her risk of default (the eighth chapter has more on how credit scoring is now evolving). FICO scores provide a simple way of categorizing end borrowers and are used by lenders, ratings agencies, and investors to assess the credit quality of the people who take out the mortgages that provide the raw material of securitization. In particular, guidelines established

in the 1990s by Fannie Mae and Freddie Mac, America's two housing-finance giants, established that anyone who scored below a
FICO score of 620 should be regarded as especially risky. That number survived as an underwriting rule of thumb after the private-label
securitization market took off. A 620 FICO score became a heuristic that was used by participants all along the securitization chain
to determine just how much extra attention needed to be given to
the borrowers. It acted in a similar way to the left-most digit on the
odometer and generated similar discontinuities.

An excellent 2008 academic paper by Benjamin Keys and three
coauthors demonstrated the effect of the 620 cutoff score during the
housing boom. The paper's hypothesis ran as follows: If it was easier
to securitize mortgages above this 620 threshold, that would have
changed the incentives of the originators of mortgages, the lenders who do the screening of individual borrowers before the loans
are packaged up and sold on as mortgage-backed securities (MBS).
In particular, it would have been easier for them to sell mortgages
from borrowers who were unable to provide proper documentation
in support of their loan applications if they had FICO scores above
620. Sure enough, the number of "low-documentation" loans that
were securitized increased dramatically as the FICO credit score
moved from below 620 to above that mark. In the sample of loans
analyzed by the authors, there was roughly a 100 percent jump at
that threshold. Investors were more prepared to forgo information
about borrowers' assets or income if they had the crutch of a specific credit score.[12]

Now imagine that you are a lender in this sort of market. Faced
with two borrowers without full documentation, one with a FICO
score of 621 and one with a FICO score of 619, which one would

you go for? The one that investors will accept without further screening, or the one that requires more qualitative, and therefore expensive, investigation—an interview to assess the applicant's job security, say? The answer should be obvious, and the consequences are also predictable. The researchers found that low-doc subprime loans just above the 620 threshold actually defaulted 20 percent more frequently than those just below the cutoff. The rule of thumb ended up making things worse for investors.

The FICO score is an important example of a heuristic sending misleading signals to the mass of investors during the recent crisis. But it had nothing on the AAA credit rating. Recall that the credit rating was a creature of the American railroad boom, an invention designed to provide investors with information on the bonds of firms that they could not personally investigate. The AAA label is the highest possible rating that the agencies bestow: Standard & Poor's defines its meaning as an "extremely strong capacity to meet financial commitments."

A 2009 paper by Manuel Adelino of the Massachusetts Institute of Technology (MIT) Sloan School of Management provides concrete evidence for just how much reassurance investors derived from this rating. A rating is only one element of the information available to investors in mortgage-backed securities: they can make their own judgments about the probability and impact of a fall in house prices, for example. To the extent that they use other sources of information that should show up in the yields (interest payments) that investors demand to hold assets.[13]

By analyzing the yields on mortgage-backed securities at issuance, Adelino found that investors generally did not rely on ratings alone to price deals and that the yields they demanded at the outset turned out to be pretty good at predicting the subsequent performance of these bonds. There was one exception to this rule of investor diligence, however. The yields that were demanded by investors in AAA-rated securities had no predictive power as regards future performance. It seems that the credit rating was all the information that these investors used.

The banks themselves also fell for the AAA heuristic. Chuck Prince, the boss of Citigroup when it blew up, told America's Financial Crisis Inquiry Commission (FCIC) that it was not surprising he had no knowledge of a mere $40 billion subprime CDO position given his bank's vast balance sheet. The passage is worth reciting in full:

> Prince told the FCIC that even in hindsight it was difficult for him to criticize any of his team's decisions. "If someone had elevated to my level that we were putting on a $2 trillion balance sheet, $40 billion of triple-A-rated, zero-risk paper, that would not in any way have excited my attention," Prince said. "It wouldn't have been useful for someone to come to me and say, 'Now, we have got $2 trillion on the balance sheet of assets. I want to point out to you there is a one in a billion chance that this $40 billion could go south.' That would not have been useful information. There is nothing I can do with that, because there is that level of chance on everything."[14]

Prince may not have been the world's greatest bank executive. But he had a gift for capturing the underlying dynamics of the crisis. As far as he was concerned, the salient fact about this exposure was not the underlying portfolio—mortgages to high-risk borrowers—but the credit rating it had. That way of thinking about finance is a function of an established market, in which standardization has both made it easy for a broader universe of investors to arise and facilitated the creation of heuristics that smooth the path to poorer judgment. "The line was clear at the beginning," says one former banker who worked for a French investment bank during the 1990s and 2000s. "Whatever I sell, I should be happy to sell to my mother and to my friends. In reality, you have a budget, you are under pressure to make money, you want a bonus, and your principles get weaker. I didn't want to go into subprime, but eventually I said okay, but only if it is AAA. What I didn't do is check what AAA meant. It was not conscious dishonesty but somehow my standards got worse."

COMPETITION CAN HAVE perverse effects in many industries, but they are particularly marked in finance. Early on in my tenure as a banking correspondent, I interviewed an executive who now heads one of the world's largest banks. The subprime crisis in the United States was gathering speed, and we were talking about what had gone wrong. Almost in passing, he said that there were only two ways to raise returns in banking: increase leverage (industry jargon for debt) or go down the credit ladder. It was a throwaway remark but one that is worth remembering. Whenever the industry is growing fast, risks are likely to be rising.

These dynamics are not just at work in the world of credit. In recent years they have also transformed the world of stock exchanges. When an investor makes a decision to sell shares or buy futures, he must find a buyer or seller to complete the deal. In the old days, that was a job for traders on the floor of an exchange. In modern markets the task falls to a bit of software called a "matching engine." In the case of NYSE Euronext, which runs equities and derivatives exchanges across Europe, the matching engines are on servers in Basildon, a town just outside London. A facility in Mahwah, New Jersey, plays the same role for NYSE in North America (the difference is that the guards there are armed).

Basildon was chosen by NYSE Euronext in part because the site, once planned as a distribution warehouse for an airconditioning firm, offered proximity to London without flooding risk or being on airline flight paths. The residents of the town are not sure what goes on in the industrial building on the town's outskirts. There are no signs outside, just a perimeter of double fencing and security guards with dogs to indicate that this is not the ordinary warehouse it appears to be. But they know it is sensitive. "The people who built it all mysteriously disappeared," jokes the taxi driver who dropped me off there one spring morning, before speeding away.

The walls protecting the halls where the servers are housed are bombproof. The halls themselves—seven in total, three of them used when I visited the facility—are separate structures so that fires do not spread. There is a backup plan for everything: four fiberoptic links from London to the data center; two power feeds, plus backup generators; tanks of ice that can quickly be melted and piped around the halls if cooling systems break down.

The exchange's own servers are stacked in glass cabinets, from which lights blink and cables snake. But some servers are kept inside locked cages, far from prying eyes. These servers belong to "high-frequency traders," who make money by dipping in and out of markets at blinding speed. The servers contain the algorithms that execute their trading strategies. Putting their machines within meters of where trades actually happen—"colocating" them, in the jargon—gives these traders a tiny but vital edge over other investors. The goal behind such tactics is always to lower "latency," the time between an order being sent and its being executed. A signal transmitted by fiber-optic cables takes about 5.5 microseconds (one microsecond is a millionth of a second) to travel one kilometer. A trader on America's West Coast who colocates his servers at the NYSE's Mahwah facility 4,000-odd kilometers away can reduce two-way latency by 22 milliseconds (thousandths of a second).[15] That is around the time it takes for a honey bee to flap its wings four times and twenty times as fast as a blink of the human eye. But it is an eon in modern electronic markets—and it seems slower all the time.

Clamber up on the roof of the Basildon center, and you can see the latest technology being used to shave communication times. Small towers stick up from the roof, with microwave dishes attached. Microwave is a "line-of-sight" technology: data gets beamed through the air from one dish to another, which means it is moving in the straightest line possible, with none of the jinks and detours that fiber-optic cables take under the ground. Basildon is already connected to markets in Frankfurt via microwave; a journey that takes around 8 milliseconds on fiber-optic cables takes 4.7 milliseconds or less this way. There is talk of a network of microwave towers stretching across the Atlantic to connect London and New York as high-frequency traders strive for the nirvana of zero latency.[16]

The changing nature of the financial markets became clear to the wider world in an event that has since become known as the "flash crash." On May 6, 2010, in a 30-minute period between 2:30 p.m. and 3:00 p.m. EDT, a number of equity markets tumbled and rebounded with extraordinary rapidity. The Dow Jones Industrial Average fell by more than 5 percent in 5 minutes, before then re-covering much of its losses. Individual share prices exhibited even more bizarre behavior. Shares in Accenture, a consultancy firm with $30 billion in annual revenues, plunged from more than $40 a share to, at one point, a single cent. The official report into the events of that day found that more than twenty thousand trades across more than three hundred securities were executed at prices more than 60 percent away from their values just moments before. On those exchanges that still have traders on the floor, confusion reigned. If you have a few minutes to spare and want to listen to the sound of chaos, find an audio recording of the futures pits in Chi-cago during those moments of panic.[17]

A joint Commodity Futures Trading Commission and Securi-ties and Exchange Commission (SEC) task force that investigated the flash crash found that the primary cause of the volatility was a "fundamental" seller. To be precise, at 2:32 p.m., a mutual fund be-gan to execute an order to sell seventy-five thousand E-Mini S&P 500 futures contracts in order to hedge an existing equity exposure. Whether trying to offload these types of contract or any other as-set, a seller does not want the price to go down before its order has gone through. So the sell order uses algorithms that are designed to sell the holding without being spotted, a bit like sneaking out of a party when it's crowded. Some algorithms slice big orders into a lot of tiny ones; in the flash crash, the computers were programmed to sell more shares when there was more trading going on in the stock.

Now let's turn to the buyers. In modern equity markets, a large proportion of transactions are carried out by high-frequency traders who are acting as market makers—intermediaries who have no intention of building an investment exposure to a specific stock. The specialist market makers of old, who would buy stock from someone and then sell it on to someone else, were prepared to hold the shares for a while, even if the price moved against them in the meantime. But that model doesn't work for high-frequency market makers. These firms offer thinner bid-ask spreads (the difference between the price at which they buy and the price at which they sell) than old-style intermediaries and also have less capital on hand to absorb losses if the price moves against them. Speed is the weapon they have to manage risk, so instead of riding out shifts in price, they try to get out of positions as fast as they can.[18]

If they find a willing investor to buy, no problem. But if they cannot, they sell to the people who are always out there offering quotes—namely, other high-frequency traders. The upshot is a "hot-potato" effect, as securities churn rapidly from one trader to another. This can lead to extraordinary numbers of transactions, which is exactly what happened during the flash crash. In a 14-second period between 2:45:13 and 2:45:27, high-frequency traders swapped more than 27,000 E-Mini contracts, which accounted for almost half of the total trading volume, while buying only about two hundred additional contracts.[19]

Remember, however, that the original algorithm uses the volume of transactions as a prompt to unload shares. The increase in trading brought about by the "hot-potato" effect acted as a signal for the first algorithm to sell more stock, which moved the price down a bit further, sparking more activity by the high-frequency traders. The loop was closed.

The flash crash comprised more elements than this volume-driven downward pressure, however. The price declines brought a lot more algorithms, used by both high-frequency traders and institutional investors, into play. Some were designed to pause trading when prices moved beyond a predefined threshold so that human traders could assess what was going on in the market. Others, called stop-loss orders, sold shares as prices hit prespecified thresholds. With orders to sell entering the market, and the liquidity to buy dwindling, prices kept falling. Some trades were executed, but at ridiculous prices. As orders scoured for buyers, some found only "stub quotes," an offer to buy at stupidly low prices—a cent for an Accenture share, for example—that market makers dangled as a way of complying with their obligation to keep quoting prices to both buyers and sellers. (Stub quotes were subsequently banned by the SEC, which now requires market makers to maintain two-sided quotations within a certain band of the best available price in the market.)

High-frequency trading really began to take off in the mid-2000s, but the flash crash thrust it into the public spotlight. Coming so soon after the 2007–2008 banking crisis, the events of May 2010 also made HFT part of the wider debate about the social value of financial innovation. In the "anti" camp are those who allege that markets are being deliberately manipulated by traders with a speed advantage. A 2012 Credit Suisse research note into "bad HFT" detected patterns of activity that suggested all sorts of nefarious practices. There is "quote stuffing," in which algorithms flood the market with orders and cancellations of those orders in order to cause congestion and slow down other traders. "Layering" refers to the practice of putting in false "buy" or "sell" orders in order to create the impression of strong buying or selling pressure, thereby driving the price in whatever direction suits the trader. "Momentum Ignition" is the name given to attempts by traders to spark other algorithms into life, causing price moves that can benefit the traders' positions.[20]

Even if such malign activities are rare—the allegations are made far more frequently than the evidence is produced—institutional investors have other, better-founded, gripes. The increase in trading activity brought about by the speedsters means that fund managers have to pay additional costs for storage and electronic reporting in order to comply with regulatory requirements. HFTs are so fast that slower-moving investors can press the button to buy a stock at a certain price and find that the price has already moved against them by the time the bulk of the trade is actually executed. However much fund managers try to disguise their activities—through volume-weighted algorithms like the one used in the flash crash, for example—the high-frequency firms will spot them and trade against them. This argument was given a fresh airing with the publication in 2014 of *Flash Boys,* a best-selling book by Michael Lewis that prompted the head of the Securities and Exchange Commission to deny that markets were rigged.[21]

To their detractors, the high-frequency traders are also at the heart of a wider problem with the capital markets: short termism. High-frequency traders account for the majority of the turnover in US equity markets, and their penetration of other asset classes and other geographies is rising. These are investors who hold on to their positions for a matter of minutes, hours, or days. Their investment decisions tend to be based not on fundamental analysis of a company's prospects, but on short-term price trends. They may be fast, critics say, but they are thoughtless.[22]

Yet the academic consensus also broadly supports the contention that high-frequency traders have helped bring down transaction costs. The British government's lengthy 2012 investigation of automated trading found that liquidity had improved, bid-ask spreads had narrowed, and markets had become more efficient. Testimony delivered to the Securities and Exchange Commission in 2010 by George Sauter of Vanguard, a big fund manager, concluded that "high-frequency traders provide liquidity and 'knit' together our increasingly fragmented marketplace, resulting in tighter spreads that benefit all investors."[23] (Critics riposte that narrower spreads are illusory if the prices quoted are not the ones at which trades are actually executed.)

It is true that investors' holding periods have gone down and down in recent years, but if short termism is a problem, its roots go deeper than the arrival of the ultrafast traders: the average holding period for British shares approached eight years in the mid-1960s and had come down to around one year by the mid-1980s. The high-tech cables and cabinets in Basildon are actually part of a rather more glacial process.

Reaching a judgment on the costs and benefits of high-frequency trading, or indeed of any financial innovation, cannot be made in a historical vacuum. Lamenting the flaws of modern finance makes very little sense without asking whether things were so much better in the old days. In a 2011 paper, Josh Lerner and Peter Tufano argued that it is virtually impossible to quantify the social impact of a financial innovation because finance involves so many "externalities"—costs or benefits visited upon third parties. For example, it would be almost impossible to measure the aggregate costs and benefits of a fundamental innovation like a bank. Instead, they reckoned, a thought experiment—imagining what the world would look like without a particular innovation—might help.[24]

A world without HFTs is easy to imagine: the old world of "specialist" market makers and floor trading existed only a few years ago, so people remember it well. There is little obvious enthusiasm for returning to that model. Transaction costs were a lot higher. Big market makers used to charge 25–40 basis points to execute trades in a clunky process that involved an investor calling a broker, who got the stock ticker and went to a jobber on the floor to make the trade. Now the same thing is being done by an algorithm at 1–3 basis points.

The very same arguments about unfair advantages were being put forward in different forms in the pre-HFT era. Now the complaints are about the milliseconds HFTs gain over ordinary investors by putting their servers right next to the exchanges' data centers; then they were about the monopolistic privileges of the specialists and the advantages of being on the trading floor. Institutional investors may now complain about being forced into "dark pools" (off-exchange venues where they can deal anonymously) to avoid the high-frequency traders, but these pools existed before HFTs and were set up in part to avoid being scalped by brokers or floor traders.

Indeed, in the very early days of automation, it was the machines that needed protection from the humans. One of the pioneers of computerized trading was a firm called the Prediction Company, which was founded in 1991 in Santa Fe, New Mexico, by a couple of chaos physicists called Norman Packard and Doyne Farmer. Packard and Farmer had already worked together on a scheme to beat the house at roulette using a toe-operated computer; the Prediction Company was an equally idiosyncratic attempt to take on the biggest casino of all, the stock market, by using physics-based models to predict short-term price movements. The firm did well: it ended up being bought by UBS, and its founders became rich. But early on it kept losing money in oil contracts on one of the markets it traded on, called NYMEX, a commodities exchange. The problem echoed the complaints made against HFTs today by institutional investors: the price that the Prediction Company was shown when it placed an order was very different from the one it ended up paying. An order to buy or sell futures at a certain price consistently cost the firm way more than anticipated.[25]

It was only when a Prediction Company employee observed what was happening on the floor of NYMEX that the mystery was solved. The firm sent in its orders at the same time every day, and the traders on the floor had noticed. As the Prediction Company order came in at its usual time, the pit quieted. Once it became clear how much the firm's broker wanted to buy or sell, everyone quickly changed their quotes, selling higher or buying lower than the Prediction Company had expected. The firm soon changed its practice, slicing orders into smaller pieces that were transacted at different times of the day so other traders wouldn't notice the size of its order. It doesn't matter whether you are trading with a human or an algorithm: the financial market is no place to show your hand.

The HFT era arose in the mid-2000s in part because of concerns about how the old system worked. A probe that looked into the behavior of specialists on the New York Stock Exchange in the early 2000s alleged that these firms had been snapping up stocks from sellers and selling them at inflated prices to customers who had placed orders to buy. That gave impetus to a rule called Regulation NMS, which was passed in 2005 and took away brokers' discretion to choose the best price for their customers. Instead, they had to use the best price available from multiple exchanges, in a system that rewarded those traders with the fastest electronic systems. HFT outfits began to grab more market share from specialist firms, whose role on the floor of exchanges was gradually being made redundant by technology. The value of these specialist firms plummeted. In 2000 Goldman Sachs bought Spear, Leeds & Kellogg, the largest specialist firm on the New York Stock Exchange, for $6.5 billion; as of April 2014, Goldman was reportedly hawking the unit for sale at a mere $30 million.[26]

LOOKED AT THROUGH a historical prism, the HFT era takes on a different appearance. The problem with HFT, as with so many of the innovative areas of finance, is not the initial idea. The old system was deeply flawed. The problem with HFT is, rather, that the unchecked logic of competition has increased the risk and potential severity of sudden market crashes. It is true that the biggest one-day fall in the history of the Dow Jones Industrial Average—a drop of almost 23 percent—happened way back on Black Monday in October 1987. But the speed with which things can go wrong is new and frightening. The flash crash is the most obvious example of how quickly the market can spiral out of control when algorithms interact.

Self-interest ought to ensure that the HFTs and other algorithmic traders manage risk robustly. There are few industries where it is possible to go out of business in a matter of seconds and minutes, and their own capital is at risk, after all. But one of the most important lessons of the past few years is that finance suffers from a "collective-action" problem, in which it may make sense for institutions to take a certain path of action, but the costs of going it alone are considered too high. The race to get faster in the world of high-frequency trading is one example: an HFT firm cannot afford to be too slow if it wants to snap up orders looking to be fulfilled. Pay is another: banks badly need to cut costs, but no one wants to be the first to drop their wages. This self-destructive dynamic is exemplified by the infamous quote that Citigroup's Chuck Prince gave a *Financial Times* reporter in the summer of 2007. "As long as the music is playing, you've got to get up and dance," he said. "We're still dancing." Nothing better captures the pressure that managers of publicly listed firms are under to pursue moneymaking opportunities, however risky, than the jiving Prince. When a market is really on a tear, the misgivings of risk managers tend to get trampled. "If you think something is wrong as a quant but the business is going well, you don't get listened to," says one mathematician with a past in the industry.[27]

Competition can easily lead firms to cut corners. Doyne Farmer, one of the founders of the pioneering Prediction Company, is now teaching at Oxford University and is far more circumspect about the benefits of electronic trading than he once was. One of the things he worries about, for example, is the pressure on high-frequency traders to simplify code. Shorter code increases speed, but it is also dumber: there isn't the luxury of inserting "if, then" clauses to instruct the algorithm to check whether the markets are in free fall, for example.

The regulators have belatedly woken up to the dangers that an automated, blindingly fast financial market brings. The flash crash underlined the importance of circuit breakers for single stocks, pauses in trading on exchanges that are triggered by a predefined movement in prices. A suspension in trading gives the humans a chance to catch up with the algorithms and think about what is going on. Germany has introduced a law that, among other things, imposes "order-to-trade ratios" designed to stop HFTs from sending out excessive numbers of orders for every transaction that they do. All this attention is encouraging the industry to smarten up its act. Everyone talks about the need for top-notch controls before and after trades are made. The back office has become sexy. Even so, there is still a gap between what the traders are capable of and the safety settings of the market. "We are in that period where the market has to catch up with us," says one trader.

HIGH-FREQUENCY TRADERS are not alone in outpacing the market in which they participate. When a financial technology or a product really takes off, the surrounding infrastructure often fails to keep pace. It is a pattern that is observable in all sorts of markets. The front office sells and sells; the back office struggles to cope. The money is flowing, but it is relying on jerrybuilt plumbing.

In today's capital markets, the problem is keeping pace with the latest developments in automation. In the late 1960s, the problem was keeping up with the paperwork. As trade volumes soared, so did the amount of bookkeeping that needed to be done to reconcile end-of-day positions and to document the transfers of share ownership. The result was known as the "paper crunch," an enormous pileup of documentation that prompted the Securities and Exchange Commission to shorten the trading day in order to give people more time to clear the backlog. A 1973 report by the New York Stock Exchange found that three out of ten investors had experienced lost or late-delivered securities.[28]

The market of credit-default swaps provides a more recent example of an infrastructure struggling to cope with rapid growth. By the mid-2000s, increasing harmonization of CDS contracts had made it much easier for contracts to be transferred to another party. Trading volumes soared, and once again the back office was swamped—in the words of one observer, it was "some way behind the elephant with a particularly small shovel trying to clear up all the shit."

One worry was an enormous backlog of unconfirmed trades, which in the event of a default would have left buyers of protection without proof of purchase. In September 2005 Tim Geithner, later the treasury secretary but then the head of the New York Federal Reserve Bank, summoned the broker dealers to his Wall Street headquarters and knocked heads together. "Everyone knew that it was a paper mess, but no one wanted to sign up to a single standard," recalls one participant in that meeting. After Geithner's intervention the industry began moving toward electronic confirmations and data repositories to record trades, and the backlogs started to reduce. By the time the 2007–2008 crisis hit, the CDS market functioned pretty efficiently, at least in an operational sense. The process for settling CDS claims after Lehman Brothers went bust, in particular, passed off more smoothly than expected.

In one crucial respect, however, the infrastructure for CDSs failed horribly: the unnoticed accumulation by the American International Group, an insurer turned derivatives trader, of huge potential liabilities as it flogged protection against default on mortgage-backed securities. Although the 2005 intervention did a lot of good, it did not deal properly with over-the-counter trades, the bit of the market where AIG was operating. AIG was allowed to take on a lot of risk without posting enough collateral until it was suddenly asked for unaffordable amounts and had to be bailed out by the US taxpayer.

Its failure has prompted another infrastructural overhaul, and not just in credit derivatives. Records of trades across all the big classes of derivatives will be collected and stored, so the chances of anyone building up a big undisclosed position should be sharply reduced. Efforts are being made to improve the way in which the posting of collateral—a kind of deposit that increases when the risks of default do—is managed and recorded.

That is good, but the pattern is disturbing. When money stands to be made, finance surges in that direction, both mutating to fit each niche that offers opportunity and standardizing so that things can get done ever faster. The front office strains at the leash, while the back office just strains. Only a near miss, or something worse, seems to prompt a response. And even then, it is hard to rein things back. I recall one conversation with an extremely smart Wall Street executive about the dangers of high-frequency trading after the flash crash had happened. "Are faster computers socially useful?" he asked rhetorically. "I don't know, but I know I still want them."

The themes we have touched on in this chapter explain how it is that financial innovations can sour. As markets develop, they attract less specialized investors. These investors rely less on their own analysis, more on heuristics and the analysis of others. As growth gathers momentum, competition drives firms to try to maximize their sources of advantage—whether that is pricing a little bit more tightly or nudging speeds up another notch. This is a stylized process, of course: not every market follows this path. But it suggests that demonizing financial innovations is the wrong lesson to draw from recent failures. Ingenuity is fine; it is the established bits of finance that cause the trouble. In fact, the next chapter takes the argument one stage further. Innovation is essential in order to change the established bits of finance for the better. And no area of the industry is bigger than property.

CHAPTER 3

THE MOST DANGEROUS ASSET IN THE WORLD

Sean Oldfield's first brush with the world of mortgages ended with bullets thudding into the ground around him. The Australian had resigned from a London-based job with Macquarie, an Australian investment bank, in 2002 with ambitions of competing in the 2004 Athens Olympics at judo. That dream died when he realized he would get knocked out in the first round, if he managed to get there at all.

Kicking around Europe with a bit of money, time on his hands, and a financial background, Oldfield read an article about the Russian mortgage market. This was still a very young industry. It was a little more than a decade since the Soviet Union had been dissolved; as part of their program of shock therapy, Russia's reformers had to create a private housing market from scratch. The amount of money being thrown at Russian housing was still paltry. Oldfield, an enterprising sort, scented opportunity and decided to head to Moscow to see if he could set up a business in housing finance.

Russia was a wild market in more ways than one. To do business in the capital back then, Oldfield needed a *krysha,* or "roof"— slang for a group that could offer Mafia-style protection from other criminal groups. His partners found him a possible *krysha,* but when he went to speak with them, Oldfield was unconvinced they could really offer him shelter. He called them up later that day to tell them so.

That was a mistake. That night the disgruntled gang members seized Oldfield and bundled him into a small, enclosed square in central Moscow, where they fired bullets into the earth around his feet. He escaped by jumping a wall topped with razor wire—and still has the scars on his hand and leg to prove it. The aim was to scare him, not kill him. "They succeeded," he says ruefully. Oldfield abandoned his Russian adventure and headed back to London.

That first abrupt experience gave him a feel for his own levels of risk tolerance. It also educated him on how mortgage markets in general work. One feature of the housing-finance market in particular bothered him: home ownership requires both the borrowers and the lenders to take on an awful lot of risk. Borrowers must face up to the possibility of unemployment, negative equity, and rising interest rates; lenders must cope with the threat of defaulting borrowers and declining asset values.

It so happened that a friend of Oldfield's had written a report in the mid-2000s for the Australian government on mortgage markets, which contained ideas on how to address that problem. And what Oldfield has been trying to do in the years since—first in Australia and then in Britain with a new venture called Castle Trust that is backed by J. C. Flowers, a well-known private-equity firm—is immeasurably more ambitious than his Moscow enterprise. He is trying to reinvent not just the world's biggest financial asset, but by far its most dangerous.

ASK YOURSELF WHAT really lay behind the 2007–2008 crisis, and the answer is not out-of-control financial wizardry. Banking systems were propelled to the brink not just in the United States, but in many other countries, too, such as Spain, Ireland, and Britain. Banks in these countries were not innovating madly: the securitization markets were nowhere near as advanced in Europe as they were in the United States. If you look across the countries most embroiled in the financial crisis, the common denominator is property. And the financial instrument that is found at scene after scene is the humble mortgage. Could it be that the real lesson to be drawn from recent financial history is that the industry suffered from too little innovation, not too much?

The chances are very high that when we next suffer a big financial meltdown, housing will be implicated. Why should that be? One reason is its sheer scale. It absorbs more wealth than any other financial asset, certainly in the rich world. Buying a house is easily the largest transaction of most people's lives. The aggregate value of property held by American households in the peak house-price year of 2006 was $22.7 trillion, their biggest single asset by a wide margin (pension-fund reserves were next, at $12.8 trillion). The amount of mortgage debt in the United States almost doubled between 2001 and 2007, to $10.5 trillion. In Britain the sum total of every residential property in 2012 was a shade under £6 trillion, which (roughly) works out at an average of £96,500 for every person in the country. Globally, the *Economist*'s most recent best guess was that residential property in the rich world as a whole was worth about 126 percent of the rich countries' combined GDP in 2010. Whatever the precise number, property is so big an asset that when capital starts to slosh around, it is likely to absorb a lot of that money, and when something goes wrong the effects will be serious.[1]

As well as being hefty, property has some particularly dangerous characteristics. This is an asset that thrives on debt. Most people do not borrow to buy shares and bonds, and if they do, the degree of leverage usually hovers around half the value of the investment. By contrast, in many housing markets buyers routinely take on loans worth 90 percent or more of the value of the property.

The particular genius of the mortgage is to put the unaffordable within reach of the masses. The amounts of money involved in buying a house are just too great for people to plow their own money in as equity: the median house price in the United States is around $220,000. Debt enables people to bridge that gap, which is not just the simple gap between the money they have and the money they need, but the gap between the money they earn now and the income they will earn in the future.[2]

But debt is also risky. First, it is a fixed obligation: it does not flex to suit changing circumstances. Second, debt magnifies swings in underlying values: the greater the amount of debt, the greater the capacity for trouble. Imagine you are buying a house that costs $200,000 and put down a deposit of 20 percent, or $40,000. The amount you borrow from the bank is $160,000. Now imagine you manage to sell the same house a couple of years later for $220,000. After paying off your loan of $160,000 and getting back your initial deposit of $40,000, the amount of money you have made is $20,000. That represents a tidy nominal return of 50 percent on your initial deposit.[3]

Not bad, but nowhere near as good as if you put down a smaller deposit of 10 percent, or $20,000, and taken out a bigger mortgage of $180,000. Now when you sell the house, you have still gained the same absolute amount of $20,000, but you have done so without putting as much of your own money at risk. The return on your deposit has zoomed to a superb 100 percent, all thanks to the magic of leverage.

The trouble, as Americans have discovered in droves, is that leverage magnifies downswings as well as upswings. In the initial example above, a 10 percent fall in the value of a $200,000 house still leaves our more cautious home buyer with $20,000 of his own money, or equity, in the house. He can sell the house, pay off the debt, and still walk away with 50 percent of his initial deposit. But in the second example, the same downward move in prices wipes out the entire deposit. In the run-up to the crisis, of course, people were often putting down much less than a 10 percent deposit. With only a tiny sliver of their own capital to protect them, and in some cases not even that, many American home owners were quickly pushed into negative equity when property prices fell: in other words, the amount they owed the bank was more than the value of their own home.

Being under water on other financial assets is not pleasant, but it is at least possible to calibrate a response. When stock prices fall, for instance, borrowers can sell some of the shares to raise whatever is needed to keep their heads above water. There is no equivalent with property: you can't decide to sell off your spare bedroom and keep the rest of the house. There are only two options: keep paying the mortgage and hope that prices rise again, or get rid of the mortgage.

Another reason to fear property is the behavioral flaws it uncovers. First of all, property has the unusual characteristic of being both something to consume and an asset to invest in. There is not much of use you can do with a share certificate except frame it. But you can both live in your house and make money from it. This mixture of motives can be toxic for financial stability. If housing were like any other consumer good, rising prices should eventually dampen demand. But since it is also seen as a financial asset, higher values are a signal to buy.

In addition, buying a house is an emotional decision as well as a financial one. There is not much point in babbling on about historic price-to-rents ratios if your partner is already mentally redecorating the house. For many young men in China, there is not much chance of landing a partner if you don't have a house to your name. That makes it likelier that people will pay over the odds.

Something as variable as the weather can also affect people's decision making. In a 2012 paper, a quartet of economists looked at something called "projection bias," the tendency for people to assume that their future tastes will resemble their current ones. The theory of projection bias suggests that consumers will assign more value to a house with a swimming pool if they see it when the weather is warm. That is irrational: since houses are generally lived in for long periods of time, through cold snaps and warm spells, the weather shouldn't affect prices. But sure enough, a house with a pool that goes under contract in the summertime sells for 0.4 percentage points more than the same house in the wintertime.[4]

Once house prices start to rise, the momentum can build up quickly. The price of residential property is set locally by the latest transactions. The value of any particular home, and the amount that can be borrowed against it, is largely determined by whatever a similar house nearby sells for. One absurd bid can push up prices for a lot of people. Even the rational buyer has an incentive to get into the market when prices are on a tear. The amount of space that people need increases predictably over time as they find partners and have children; it makes sense to buy early in order to protect themselves against the risk of future price increases that would make houses unaffordable.

When prices start going up, another behavioral bias starts to kick in. The "availability heuristic" captures the propensity of people to assess situations by referring to examples that come readily to mind. A 2008 paper by Hugo Benitez-Silva, Selcuk Eren, Frank Heiland, and Sergi Jiménez-Martín used the Health and Retirement Study, a biennial survey of Americans over the age of fifty, to compare people's estimates of the value of their homes with actual values when a sale took place. The authors found that home owners overestimate the value of their homes by an average of 5–10 percent. Those who had bought during good times tended to be more optimistic in their valuations, whereas those who had bought during a downturn were more realistic.[5]

Property is also prey to a bias known as "money illusion," which is the tendency for people to concentrate on nominal changes in prices as opposed to real values that take inflation into account. The difference between the value of the house when you bought it and the value of the house when you sold it can sound very alluring, particularly over long periods of time. The average house price in Britain at the start of 1975 was £10,388; in September 2013, despite the housing downturns of the 1990s and the recent crisis, it had shot up to £170,918, a gain of more than 1,500 percent.[6]

But put those figures into real prices, and things look much less impressive. In inflation-adjusted terms, £10,388 was worth about £84,340 in today's money, which translates into a gain of just 100 percent over an almost 40-year period. It is a similarly unimpressive story in other countries: the record of price increases over the 110-year period from 1900 to 2010 shows an average yearly increase of 1 percent in real terms in places as varied as the United States, Australia, France, and Norway. One of the longest continuous house-price series in the world is for properties on the Herengracht Canal in central Amsterdam: the real price level for a Herengracht property in 1992 was the same as it had been in 1646. It is true that real prices in many countries did shoot up vertiginously in the years immediately prior to the crisis, but that is the exception, not the rule.[7]

Add all these things together, and it becomes clear why property is a paradise for students of behavioral finance, the idea that psychology can explain investors' systematic errors. In a 2013 lecture to the American Economics Association, Edward Glaeser, a Harvard academic, described nine different episodes of property bubbles in the United States, from a land boom in Alabama in 1819 to the skyscraper craze in New York in the 1920s. He revealed a consistent failure to remember a very basic rule of economics: supply and demand. The boom in Alabama in 1815–1819 was driven by the belief that its cotton-growing soil and English demand would deliver endless profits; instead, more cotton was grown, driving prices down and land values with it. The enthusiasm for skyscrapers in Manhattan in the 1920s obscured an obvious problem, that the scope to build upward created the potential for a vast oversupply of space, which duly materialized in the 1930s.[8]

IF BEHAVIORAL FLAWS help explain why ordinary people get property wrong, shouldn't the professionals do a better job of parsing the risks? In fact, banks and fund managers seem to be just as prone to mistakes. From the most recent crisis in 2007–2008 to Spain in the 1970s, Sweden and Japan in the early 1990s, and a host of Southeast Asian economies in the late 1990s, banks have historically tended to get into trouble when a housing cycle peaks and prices fall.

One reason is that it is very difficult to profit if you believe that property prices are too high. In the equity markets, you can go "short" by borrowing the shares in question from existing owners for a fee; you then sell those shares in the expectation they will fall and buy them back once the price has fallen. The difference between the price you sold at and the price you bought at is profit. But how on earth are you supposed to borrow a house in order to sell it? Investors who thought that America's housing market was headed for a cliff could find ways to express this sentiment by buying protection on mortgage-backed securities through credit-default swaps, but there are many easier trades in the world to execute. Without a simple way to go short on housing, there was less downward pressure to mitigate the exuberance of a boom.

The perception of safety also makes property dangerous. A property loan is "secured"—it is backed by a tangible asset that will retain some value if the borrower defaults. That makes it safer than an unsecured loan, where there is no collateral for a lender to grab if things go wrong. Indeed, one of the bigger ironies of the property bubble was that many lenders and investors who had been suckered by the mirage of dot-com riches thought they were being relatively prudent by concentrating on housing.

Although collateralized lending offers a degree of protection to the individual lender, it has an unfortunate systemic effect: the feedback loop between asset prices and the availability of credit. In a boom, rising property prices increase the value of the collateral held by banks, which makes them more willing to extend credit. Easier credit means that buyers can extend themselves further to get the property they want, driving up house prices further. The loop operates in reverse, too. As prices fall, lenders tighten their standards, forcing potential buyers to opt out of the market and speeding up the decline in prices.

The comparative safety of secured lending is embedded in the rules on bank capital. Bank capital is shorthand for the equity funding that banks get from shareholders. Equity provides the most important margin of safety for the financial system, because it absorbs the impact of losses (unlike debt, which needs to be repaid to lenders whether a bank has sustained a loss or not). There is a simple way of setting the amount of capital that banks must raise. Called a leverage ratio, it expresses the minimum level of equity as a simple percentage of banks' assets. A leverage ratio of 3 percent, which is the minimum specified in the latest set of Basel accords on bank capital, requires a bank with $100 billion in assets to have at least $3 billion of equity. But a leverage ratio takes no account of the riskiness of the assets: a bank would need to have $3 billion in equity whether it was invested in boring US Treasuries or something much more daring like high-yield emerging-market bonds. That seems wrong: if equity is the bit of the balance sheet that is supposed to absorb losses, shouldn't there be more of it when the risks are higher?[9]

So the regulators have another way of determining capital, which measures the riskiness of assets. What happens is that assets that are considered safe are assigned a lower dollar value than they have in reality. These calculations make a very big difference to the size of banks' balance sheets. As a random but fairly typical example, the value of JPMorgan Chase's assets in mid-2012 stood at more than $2.2 trillion before adjusting for risk, but plunged to just over $1.3 trillion when assets were risk weighted. That makes a big difference to the amount of actual capital that banks have to raise from shareholders. The leverage ratio of the ten largest banking firms in the United States was only 2.8 percent in 2007, even though their risk-based capital ratio remained around 11 percent.[10]

Property looks very attractive in this sort of environment. Risk weights are driven by a lot of things, but two of the biggest factors are "probability of default," which measures the likelihood of not being paid back on a loan, and "loss given default," which measures how much money a creditor is going to get back if a borrower does fail to repay. The loss-given-default calculation clearly favors secured over unsecured assets: you can get back more money if you have an asset to claim and sell. And that means a lower risk weight for property than for something like corporate loans.

Risk weights are not the only determinants of business mix, of course: assets that are riskier should attract a higher return, for one thing. But because banks generally prefer to fund themselves with debt rather than equity, lower risk weights provide a big extra incentive for lenders to throw more money toward property than toward other assets such as loans to small and medium-size businesses.

To this flammable mixture, politicians are prone to adding another dose of paraffin. Until the 2007–2008 crisis, administration after administration had a policy of promoting home ownership in the United States. If you want to get people into homes of their own, then you have to find a way for them to fund the purchase. From the founding of Fannie Mae in 1938, in a scheme designed to create a secondary market for home mortgages, to the signing of the American Dream Downpayment Act of 2003 by President George W. Bush, government helped create the financing infrastructure that propelled the US home-ownership rate ever higher. More than that, it created a narrative that made it a matter of natural justice to own a home. This is what President Bush said when he signed that tellingly named act:

> I am here today because we are taking action to bring many thousands of Americans closer to owning a home. Our Government is supporting homeownership because it is good for America; it is good for our families; it is good for our economy. One

of the biggest hurdles to homeownership is getting money for a downpayment. This administration has recognized that, and so today I'm honored to be here to sign a law that will help many low-income buyers to overcome that hurdle and to achieve an important part of the American Dream.

Private enterprises could not create this kind of narrative on their own: their interests are commercial and therefore immediately suspect. But add in the power of the presidency and a sprinkling of star-spangled rhetoric, and the subprime mortgage became an instrument of equality. "You had greed and justice marching together, and that's a hard thing to stop" is how one Wall Streeter puts it.

All of these distortions around property help to explain why a fast-growing financial sector appears to be bad for aggregate productivity growth. Growth in GDP per head seems to be negatively correlated with the financial sector's share of total employment (that is, the more bankers there are, the less quickly we grow richer). A 2013 paper by Stephen Cecchetti and Enisse Kharroubi of the Bank for International Settlements suggests that part of the reason is that finance grows by directing disproportionate amounts of capital to sectors such as property. A tangible asset like a house, an office block, or a warehouse is easier to value and easier to pledge against financing; it also raises recovery rates in the event of a borrower default. When finance is growing quickly, it does so by directing capital to where it flows most naturally, not to where it may be used most productively. And more often than not, as we saw in the idea of "false substitutes" from Chapter 2, the most natural place for money to flow is where it feels safest.[11]

Time and again, however, the safety of property proves illusory. When borrowers default and their houses are sold off for less than the value of the outstanding loan, their lenders start to take losses. And because property is such a big part of banks' balance sheets and banks are also heavily indebted, losses in housing have the capacity to erode their own thin layers of equity. "Banks are leveraged and property is leveraged, so there is double leverage," sums up a former chief risk officer of HSBC. "That is why a property crash is a problem for the banks." Some regulators have noticed the repetitiveness of financial history. "We do not want to fight the last war" is how one European banking regulator put it privately, referring to property busts, "but the fact is that we keep fighting the same war over and over."

IT IS COMMONPLACE to think of the property market as having suffered from too much innovative thinking. It is true that a lot of effort went into enabling consumers and investors to take on more and more property-related debt. But all of the pitfalls of property described above argue for more fresh thinking, not less.

Sean Oldfield's answer to the problem of double leverage is to share out the risks in one of two ways. The first way is to use a concept called "shared equity," so that the bank also takes an ownership share in the house. At the moment, most people face two choices when it comes to their accommodation: they can either rent a property or go a very long way into debt in order to own one. "There is no way of fractionally owning something," says Oldfield. A mortgage entails an obligation to repay that remains whatever happens to house prices or to interest rates. One of Oldfield's childhood memories from Australia is of accompanying his mother to the bank manager at a time when interest rates had soared and the strain of keeping up with the mortgage threatened their ability to stay in the family home. Even then, the mismatch between a salary that moves annually in small increments and a cost that could spike suddenly and dramatically struck the young Sean as unfair.

Companies do not restrict their room for maneuver in this way. They issue a mixture of debt and equity and some hybrid instruments in between that give them more flexibility. When profits fall, dividends can be cut. When losses mount, shareholders take the strain. Oldfield wants home owners, in effect, to issue equity, too, reducing the amount of money they have to pay out and sharing in the gains and losses caused by house-price movements.

Castle Trust, the British mortgage venture he has set up with backing from J. C. Flowers, offers a product called a partnership mortgage, in which the firm lends 20 percent of a property's value but asks for no monthly interest or capital repayments. Instead, when the home owner sells up, he or she has to repay the original loan amount and give Castle Trust a 40 percent share of any house-price gain. Conversely, if prices have gone down, Castle Trust will shoulder a 20 percent share of the losses.

The idea of shared equity is not new to Castle Trust. The business that Oldfield founded in Australia was based on the same idea. That firm was based on a fund-management model in which money was raised from investors, deployed in mortgages, and the proceeds eventually passed back to investors. Castle Trust started out in the same way, until Oldfield had an epiphany watching television with his wife one night. Off went the television, out came

the whiteboard (the home accessory of choice for the financial professional), and on it he sketched out an entirely different way of
running the business.

The new model is based on structuring the balance sheet in
order to achieve the second form of risk sharing: between Castle
Trust's borrowers and its lenders. Recall that one of the pernicious
properties of debt is that it is an obligation to pay back the loan and
interest no matter what. That hurts home owners in a downturn,
which is why shared equity is an attractive idea. But it also hurts
banks when there is a property bust, because banks fund much of
their own lending activity by borrowing. The losses that banks take
on the asset side of the balance sheet do not reduce the liabilities
that they owe. Shared equity does not help this problem; indeed, it
can exacerbate it.

People in the financial markets sometimes liken a bank's mortgage book to a "put option." A put option is a contract in which a
buyer has the right to sell an asset at a particular price by a certain
date, and the seller of the put has the obligation to buy the asset if
this right is exercised. Writing put options hands you a limited upfront payment but entails a much bigger risk if prices plummet and
you end up having to buy an asset at above-market prices. To some,
that is similar to the kind of trade that banks make when they loan
money on a house. If house prices go up, the bank doesn't make any
more money from the loan. If the market goes down and defaults
start to occur, the bank starts to own assets in a declining market.

Oldfield's idea was to construct a balance sheet that rebalances
automatically. On the asset side are mortgages, which will lose or
gain money if house prices go down or up. Funding these mortgages

are investment products that track a national house-price index, so that the amount of money investors get back will also go up or down if prices rise or fall. If house prices fall, therefore, Castle Trust's assets and liabilities should both drop. Things are not quite that simple, of course, because there may be a difference between the national house-price index that Castle Trust's funding is tied to and the actual portfolio of mortgages that the firm writes. It is easy to imagine the index and the Castle Trust loan book moving at different speeds and perhaps even in different directions. Oldfield's task is to try to mimic the composition of the national index as the business builds, so that he doesn't have too many mortgages on a particular type of property or in a specific region.

The Castle Trust model is a radical break from the norm. Oldfield's initial conception of the business has already collided with the reality of the British housing market, where prices have again been rising rapidly. New home owners have so far been unwilling to take out mortgages that give up a thick slice of any capital gains in return for a bit of insurance against the worst. Instead, the growth in the business has come from people remortgaging, where the firm again issues an equity loan without interest or capital repayments for 20 percent of a property's value and takes a 40 percent slice of house-price gains in return, but does not share in the downside. That has proved an attractive proposition for buy-to-let investors and for older home owners who have a lot of equity locked up in their house and want to turn a slice of it quickly into cash ("liquefy it," in the jargon). The purists' idea of a market for house-price insurance is not yet reality, Oldfield acknowledges, although he still insists its day will come.

In the meantime, however, there is a lot still to like about what Oldfield is doing. The idea of a balance sheet that is agnostic about the direction of house prices is extremely powerful. Other banks are making huge unhedged bets on house prices. When they fall sharply enough to hurt mortgage lenders, bad things tend to happen to everyone. Any system that neutralizes banks' property exposures is one worth pursuing.

And Castle Trust also addresses an important problem when prices are rising fast: how to get onto the housing ladder. Rising prices may seem like a good thing for the economy as a whole, but they involve a transfer of wealth from people who do not already own homes to those who do. Dearer housing makes it harder for the wannabe property owner to afford a home: in 1977 the average age of a first-time buyer in Britain was twenty-seven, by 2007 it was thirty-four, and in 2011 it had risen to thirty-seven. Again, the market has provided a different answer to this problem than Oldfield had anticipated. He had assumed that the investment product would be the solution. If they can invest in housing via an index, then non–home owners can benefit from rising home prices, too, and not see the prospect of home ownership recede ever further into the distance. In practice, however, the shared-equity mortgage is how people are solving the problem. Older home owners with tons of equity in their own houses and children to lift onto the housing ladder can unlock money and hand the cash to their offspring for use as deposits on their own homes.[12]

This is not an ideal solution: it favors families that are already sitting on a lot of housing wealth and increases housing demand by providing a new stream of buyers with an instant means of purchasing. But it also increases the amount of equity funding in the mortgage market, and that is entirely welcome.

Oldfield's model is less suited to the United States, where the continued availability of tax deductions on mortgage payments makes it hard for an equity-financing model to fly. But finance's innovators have been busy there, too, capitalizing on the burgeoning rental market. Home-ownership rates in America dropped from 69.2 percent at its peak in 2004 to 64.3 percent in the third quarter of 2014, its lowest rate since 1994. Plans for reforming Fannie Mae and Freddie Mac will have the effect of further shrinking the supply of mortgage credit in the United States. Many people are now locked out of the housing market because their credit scores were damaged during the bust.

That has started to draw institutional money into the single-family-home rental sector. In November 2013 Invitation Homes, the single-family rental unit of Blackstone, a big private-equity firm, sold the first ever "single-family rental" bond. Unlike mortgage-backed securities, in which the income that goes to investors is made up of pooled mortgage payments, a rental bond bundles together the payments that tenants make to landlords. Blackstone's $479 million issue was serviced by the rental payments on more than three thousand homes in Arizona, California, Florida, and elsewhere. The idea of rental bonds is another that deserves a thumbs-up. The obsession with home ownership led to disaster; a funding mechanism that increases the availability of rental properties is a good thing.

Yet despite these innovative efforts, housing remains an asset that is characterized principally by a dearth of fresh thinking—overprivileged by regulators and politicians, under-thought by mainstream financial institutions. For all the talk of the newfangled products that blew up the world's financial system, the one that really caused the trouble was the most familiar one of all.

Property also offers a lens for thinking about how finance in general can be most productive in the future. The housing boom developed in part because of behavioral flaws in the way that people manage money and risk; might those flaws be harnessed for more constructive ends? The housing bust underlined the danger of carrying too much debt; just like Oldfield, financial entrepreneurs are now thinking about ways to increase the use of equity as a source of capital in other asset classes, too. Property is the financial system's point of greatest vulnerability, not least because it is a long-term asset funded by shorter-term borrowing; how might the banking system be adapted to address these fragilities? And Western economies were happy to use housing wealth to gloss over fundamental problems in the distribution of wealth, the strength of the welfare system, and the capacity of older people to support themselves; the end of the housing boom reinforces the need for new thinking on all these issues.

This part of the book has argued that finance has solved great problems in the past by innovating, that the industry's flaws emerge after ideas have become established, and that a lack of innovation ought to worry people more than its presence. In the next part, we look at the shape of financial innovation today—the entrepreneurs who are now driving finance forward and some of the issues they are trying to solve.

PART II
A Force for Good

CHAPTER 4

SOCIAL-IMPACT BONDS AND THE SHRINKING OF THE STATE

Innovative Finance Expert Saves Struggling Zoo by
Letting Guests Feed, Eat the Animals
—THE *ONION*

Martinez Sutherland is in his midforties and has been in and out of British prisons since he was fourteen. He makes no excuses for his behavior. "I can't blame it on my parents," he says. "I was just a little villain." He has been inside for years at a time, including a five-year sentence for his role in a drug-related killing. "My whole life has been dogshit alley."

The prospect of someone like Sutherland really turning his life around may seem slim, but his odds have been improved by two twists of fate. The first was that his most recent spell in prison—for spitting at a policeman after an altercation ("I deserved to go to jail")—was a short sentence of under a year. The second was that he was jailed in Peterborough, an unremarkable city in eastern England. Those two details in a biography of crime sound minor, but they meant that Sutherland qualified to take part in a prisoner-rehabilitation program that is attracting attention around the world because of the way it is being financed.

Peterborough is home to the world's first "social-impact bond." A SIB works by using private investors to fund social programs, particularly ones that are designed to intervene in people's lives before they go seriously off-track. The investors are paid back from public funds, with a return on top, if targets are met. The theory is that successful projects ought to translate into savings for the public purse, which can be used to pay investors without any additional public spending.

The Peterborough pilot, which kicked off in 2010, is focused on prisoner rehabilitation. Money from seventeen private investors, mainly philanthropic organizations and charitable trusts, is being used to fund social organizations that work with male prisoners leaving Peterborough prison after serving short sentences—a cohort that included Martinez Sutherland when he was released in August 2013. This is a group that falls between the cracks of formal government services. Ex-inmates who have been inside for less than a year have traditionally gotten very little statutory support from the probationary authorities. Reoffending rates are extremely high: more than 60 percent of them offend again within a year of release.

The program measures a single outcome: the number of convictions in the cohort group twelve months after leaving prison. Fewer convictions mean less spending by the state. The reoffending rate in Peterborough is compared with recidivism rates in a control group of prisoners elsewhere in Britain with a similar profile. If they are sufficiently superior to the comparison group, Britain's Ministry of Justice and another public body called the Big Lottery Fund will make payments to investors.

Young though they are, SIBs are a great response to the question of whether financial innovation can ever be useful. They are one possible answer to the squeeze on government spending in rich countries. They are a way of channeling money to organizations that deliver the best outcomes. And they show how some of the most critical concepts in finance—from transferring risk to making claims on future streams of cash—can be used to do good.

SIR RONALD COHEN is the man who has done more than anyone else to get social-impact bonds off the ground. Sir Ronald made his name getting a different financial industry started. In 1972, at the age of twenty-six, he cofounded the firm that became Apax Partners. By the time of his departure, in 2005, Apax had grown into one of Europe's biggest private-equity firms, with more than $40 billion under management.

Silver haired, liberal minded, politically connected, and unfailingly courteous, Sir Ronald is the most urbane of buyout barons. His passion at Apax was cultivating entrepreneurs and enabling them to bring their ideas to fruition; the boom-era business of taking on ever more debt to buy up established companies isn't really him. Having arrived in Britain in the 1950s as a Jewish refugee from Egypt, he has also long worried about the gaps opening up in society between the haves and have-nots. A warning he gave in 2007 on the potential for violence as a result of rising inequality attracted a lot of public attention.

Sir Ronald's interests in entrepreneurship and social inequality came together in the field of social investment, now sometimes called "impact investing"—the allocation of capital to ventures that offer a mixture of social and financial benefits. A SIB provides this sort of blended return. Investors in the Peterborough pilot, for example, can expect a return of up to 13.5 percent if all the reoffending targets are met, nice enough but still below the returns that an investor might normally expect to make in an instrument this risky. The compensation for this shortfall in financial returns is the social impact that the initiative delivers.

Sir Ronald has been laboring in the area for long enough to be known as the father of social investment. (There are plenty of fathers but few mothers in this book: finance does not do well in promoting women.) In 2000 he chaired a "Social Investment Task Force" on behalf of the then Labour government. Its remit was to look at the problem of poverty, but to do so with an eye on how entrepreneurship might help. As Sir Ronald talked to leaders of social organizations in Britain and the United States, he noticed something strange: there was a lot of money stuck in charitable foundations and a lot of providers doing sterling work, but the two weren't meeting. Just as the idea of venture capital (VC) is to connect money with profit-seeking entrepreneurs, Sir Ronald became convinced that there was an opportunity to do the same with social entrepreneurs.

For that to happen, what would be needed was a "social-investment bank," an institution that would experiment with different products and use its balance sheet to provide capital to promising organizations. The first step in that direction was Bridges Ventures, a social-investment fund founded by Sir Ronald in 2002 that targets commercial returns but concentrates on the most deprived areas of Britain. The next step was Sir Ronald's seat on another government commission, this one looking into what could be done with unclaimed assets lying in British bank accounts. A recommendation to use a £250 million chunk of these assets to found a social-investment bank was turned down by Gordon Brown, the then Labour prime minister, who instead offered £75 million. That wasn't enough for Sir Ronald, whose response in 2007 was to set up an organization called Social Finance, with a remit to prove what a social-investment bank was capable of. He and three friends provided the money and started recruiting.

The team at Social Finance was hired to innovate, and as they started researching projects around the world, the germ of an idea emerged. Couldn't you finance nonprofits on the basis of how well they did their job, using the money that government saved through better outcomes to pay off investors? To this financing mechanism, Sir Ronald added a venture-capital twist: by having an intermediary like Social Finance assist the social organization as it went along, a transaction like this could add management skills as well as money.

The skeleton of a social-impact bond now existed on paper. A chance conversation with someone who pointed out the amount of data that already existed on prisoners steered the team at Social Finance to its first implementation: reducing rates of prisoner recidivism. So in 2010 Sir Ronald and others went to Britain's Ministry of Justice to present the idea of a £12 million social-impact bond to fund rehabilitation programs for ex-prisoners at three prisons.

As Sir Ronald tells it, the Labour justice minister at the time, Jack Straw, listened to the proposal and turned to one of his officials. "I know nothing should ever be done for the first time," he said, "but we're going to look at this." Straw's team duly did so and told the Social Finance team that they could try the idea out, but that the bond could be for only £5 million, not £12 million. They also said the bond should focus on one prison, and they wanted it to be the jail in Peterborough.

I VISITED THE SCHEME in May 2013. It was undeniably impressive. The Peterborough project is run by an umbrella group called One Service, which brings together a number of different charitable organizations with different areas of expertise, from mental health to support services for the families of prisoners. Contact with prisoners begins while they are still inside. Those who opt into the scheme (the vast majority do) are met at the gates upon release so that basic issues such as the provision of housing are properly addressed; otherwise, some prisoners reoffend immediately in order to ensure they have accommodation of some sort.

Ex-prisoners are assigned caseworkers, some of whom are ex-offenders themselves, to look after them. Volunteers provide an additional level of support to help with practicalities such as job training. The scheme has its own training initiative, providing a sixteen-week course in painting and decorating to those who want it. When I visited the training site, a group of sallow young men proudly showed off the partition wall they had been working on. Finding a job is the biggest problem, of course, and One Service also helps find work placements. Martinez Sutherland was on one such placement when I first spoke to him at the end of 2013 and living in his own place for the first time in his life. It is easy to be skeptical about his prospects, but his tone was upbeat, his voice alive with opportunity. A path out of "dogshit alley" was opening up.

The signs are also promising for the program as a whole. Results released in August 2014 showed an 8.4 percent reduction in reconvictions since the start of the program compared with the national baseline. If the scheme keeps performing like that and achieves a reduction in reconvictions of 7.5 percent or more compared with the control group, the original investors will receive a payout in 2016.

Whatever its eventual results, the real impact of the Peterborough SIB will have been to kick-start a new market. Britain is home to the greatest number of SIBs, helped along by the enthusiasm of David Cameron, the Conservative British prime minister, for an idea he calls the "Big Society." Almost no one knows what this phrase means, but if it has any substance at all, it is in the area of social investment. Under Cameron's government, Sir Ronald's old idea of a social-investment bank has become a reality: in 2012 he became the first chairman of Big Society Capital, an institution with £600 million in capital and a mandate to create a social-investment market. The number of SIBs launched or in development in Britain is now well into double digits. Each is a geek's delight: a knotty problem resolved by data and the alignment of incentives.[1]

Among Big Society Capital's investments to date is a SIB commissioned by the Essex County Council that is designed to work with troubled adolescents to prevent them from ending up in the care of the state. Keeping teenagers with their families matters hugely to their long-term prospects: a quarter of all British prisoners have been in foster care, compared with 2 percent of the population overall. The SIB will fund a program of "multisystemic therapy," an intensive intervention that works not just with the child, but also with anyone who is a big part of the child's life—from families and schools to even, on occasion, the drug dealers who supply children. Kids who stay out of foster care represent a big saving for the state: that saving will pay back investors.

Another SIB funds work by two homelessness charities in London to help get a group of some eight hundred long-term "rough sleepers" off the streets. These are people who drift in and out of the state's orbit, sometimes going into accommodation before ending up back on the pavement, often winding up in hospitals' emergency rooms. They are neither so settled into life on the streets that they live self-sufficiently nor so new to it that they can be funneled quickly into a hostel. I spent one early morning in winter tracking Kath Sims, a worker for a charity called St. Mungo's, as she checked up on some of the 415 homeless people on her list. On a street off Berkeley Square, I watched as she knelt beside a blue sleeping bag that was sandwiched snugly into a doorway. Inside was a longtime rough sleeper with a history of violence, a drug habit to feed, and a string of prison sentences. There are no quick fixes for a person with his profile. Kath needs time to build a relationship with him: stopping to say hello and roll him a cigarette is part of that process. Coaxing him into a hostel, the normal first step off the streets, is not the right approach: he'd only end up in a fight and have an eviction on his record that would make it much harder eventually to place him in permanent accommodation. Instead, the priority is to get his drug abuse under control by weaning him onto methadone. It takes time, effort, and committed funding.

Ideas for SIBs are not just coming from the public sector. The first social-impact bond to be arranged by nonprofit organizations is in the field of adoption. A group of eighteen British voluntary adoption agencies is using a SIB to fund a program to find families for hard-to-place children. Adoption is a buyer's market: wannabe parents have the pick of kids, and the cutest, youngest, and whitest children have the best chances of finding new homes. Placing siblings is a particular challenge: this is a market where people do not buy in bulk. The SIB will fund a program in which adoption agencies work on behalf of harder-to-place children by, for example, offering their adoptive parents intensive support in the first two years after placement. Payments to investors will come from the savings that accrue to local government from a successful placement.

Britain may lead the sector, but SIBs are also being developed in places as far afield as Australia and Colombia, Canada and India. Sir Ronald has chaired a G8 task force on social-impact investment, whose report in September 2014 outlined steps that governments could take to encourage the market. SIBs may even have a role to play in the Palestinian conflict. Nothing if not ambitious, Sir Ronald is hoping to organize SIBs in Israel that would provide training and job-placement assistance for Orthodox Jews and for Arabs in that country. Social Finance, the intermediary organization he set up, reckons that as many as a hundred different SIB initiatives are being explored around the world.

But if the center of gravity shifts anywhere, it will be to the United States. The first American SIB was launched in the summer of 2012 by New York City and is in the same area of prisoner rehabilitation as the Peterborough bond, working with adolescents in the city's Rikers Island facility. The investors include Goldman Sachs and the personal foundation of Michael Bloomberg, New York's billionaire former mayor.

The State of Massachusetts has two SIBs in production, one a $27 million seven-year program in the same area of prisoner recidivism; Goldman is again putting in some of the money. The state is also home to the American sister organization of Social Finance and to a "laboratory" set up by Jeffrey Liebman, a professor of public policy at Harvard University's Kennedy School of Government, which has been providing technical assistance on social-impact bonds to state authorities in New York and Massachusetts. Liebman set up the lab after looking into the Peterborough bond. Demand for his services is high. A 2013 grant enabling Liebman's team to provide advice to four more US states wound up attracting applications from twenty-eight of them.

Wall Street is also waking up to the opportunity in social investment. As well as Goldman's involvement in the sector, Bank of America applied in 2012 for a trademark on the nauseating phrase "Anything a Society Truly Wants Can Be Financed and Achieved"; the application mentions SIBs, among other things.

WHAT EXCITES PEOPLE about SIBs is their potential to channel sustainable funding to social programs that have the best outcomes. By using the mechanics of the market, social-impact bonds align the incentives of several different parties: the government entities that commission services, the social organizations that provide those services, and the investors that supply capital.

Take each in turn. Governments—or, more accurately, taxpayers—are the ones at the end of the financial chain when society fails its citizens. Helping the most marginalized members of a society is the right thing for any government to do. It is also costly. And many governments cannot afford to spend in the way they once did. The twentieth century was a story of inexorable state expansionism. Leviathan gobbled up an ever larger share of the economy in the rich world, as social safety nets, among other things, became wider and thicker. The pattern in emerging markets is likely to be the same in this century, as their citizens become richer and demand greater welfare protection.

The growth of public spending accelerated wildly in the first decade of the twenty-first century. In his excellent book *When the Money Runs Out*, Stephen King, HSBC's chief economist, points out the rapid jumps that took place between 2000 and 2012 in Western government spending: from 33.9 percent of GDP to 41.1 percent in the United States, from 36.5 percent to 48.9 percent in Britain, from 51.6 percent to 55.9 percent in France. And before you object that this rise was caused by the need to save the banks and the economies they wrecked, the financial crisis explains only some of this hike: on average, around half of these rises took place before the start of the crisis.[2]

As populations age, the chunk of public spending that is growing fastest is on such entitlements as pensions and health care. The Congressional Budget Office in the United States reckons that the total cost of entitlements such as Social Security (pensions), Medi-care (health care for the elderly), Medicaid (health care for the poor), and the subsidies involved in Obamacare will rise inexorably over the coming years, from 9.8 percent of GDP in 2013 to 13.6 percent by 2035.[3]

The problem for democratic governments is that cutting back on entitlements is both the most obvious fiscal fix and the least at-tractive politically. The easier option, as the name suggests, is to try to reduce the pot of money for "discretionary programs," where the state will not have to renegotiate guaranteed commitments to its citizens.

The SIB structure is one way of delivering more cost-effective spending in these discretionary areas because the government pays out only if specific outcomes are delivered. Investors in the Peter-borough bond get nothing if targets are not met, for example.

It is possible for the state to pay up even if savings do not ac-crue. The Peterborough program might lead to a big drop in re-conviction rates but not deliver any financial benefits to the British government if, for example, there was a week of rioting that meant the local prisons ended up more crowded than ever. The really big savings would require a large-enough rehabilitation program that entire prisons could be closed. But just as debt is a way to fund current expenditure using future earnings, a SIB is a way to pay for preventative social interventions with the future cost savings they will generate.

A SIB is an improvement on many existing state procurement processes that offer payments based on performance. Too often, the wrong things get counted. Job-training programs, for example, often focus on inputs such as the number of participants and outputs such as the number of graduates from a scheme, rather than on the numbers who secure employment. That is like measuring the number of widgets a factory produces in an hour, but not how many of them are sold.

The result is that money—a lot of money—is being pumped into programs that are not actually delivering decent results. Between 1990 and 2010, ten federal government social programs in the United States were evaluated using randomized control trials (RCTs), a method of randomly assigning people between one group whose members are receiving certain services and another group whose members are not. Measuring the difference in outcomes between the two tells you how useful a specific program is. Nine of the ten federal programs were found to have weak or no positive effects: they were a waste of taxpayers' money.[4]

Some initiatives actually end up doing harm. An American program with the sensitive name "Scared Straight" aimed to deter teenagers from a life of crime by allowing them to interact with hardened criminals in custody. The results seemed very encouraging, until RCTs gave a fuller picture of what would have happened to these kids if they had not had a chance to sit down with serial offenders. The RCTs suggested that the program increased offending rates and incurred costs for the taxpayer that were more than thirty times higher than any benefits.[5]

Even if a government applies sensible metrics and techniques like RCTs, there is another problem with pay-for-performance contracts: cash flow. Providers like One Service and St. Mungo's need to pay their employees and suppliers in order to deliver services; they cannot wait around for a payment based on how they have done. And if governments hand over the cash at the start of the contract, then taxpayers still end up spending money even if outcomes are disappointing. The promise of the social-impact-bond arrangement for governments is thus threefold: a payment structure that is based on outcomes, casts those payments into the future, and transfers the risk of wasted spending to other people.

Once you start thinking about the model, it is easy to identify all sorts of areas where more money and greater innovation are badly needed. Soldiers reentering civilian life face huge difficulties in making the transition, for example. According to America's Veterans Support Organization, nearly one in five servicemen and servicewomen returning from the conflicts in Iraq and Afghanistan have symptoms of post-traumatic stress disorder or major depression. Rates of unemployment, homelessness, and suicide among these veterans are all higher than average. This is not just a human tragedy, but also a big financial burden. A program that worked intensively with former soldiers in that process of reintegration would be a natural candidate for a SIB.

In health, programs to ensure early detection of conditions such as diabetes have the potential to realize massive savings. The American Diabetes Association puts the total cost of diagnosed diabetes in the United States in 2012 at $245 billion, of which $176 billion is put down to direct medical expenses and the rest to reduced productivity. These costs could be at least constrained if people with prediabetes, a condition in which blood glucose levels are higher than normal but have yet to reach diabetic levels, were identified and changed their diets and exercise habits in time. Again, a SIB might be one mechanism for funding early-detection programs, with governments paying out of savings from reduced incidence of type-2 diabetes.

Governments need not be the only entities to commission SIBs, however. In emerging markets, the apparatus of the state is often undeveloped; without a welfare state to speak of, there cannot be big government savings for SIB-funded programs to reap. But there is a lot of money flowing to these countries via aid organizations and national development budgets.

Michael Belinsky, an alumnus of Jeffrey Liebman's lab in Massachusetts, has formed a consultancy called Instiglio to advise on emerging-market SIBs (also known as "development-impact bonds"). One of the projects he's been working on is a SIB aimed at improving educational outcomes for marginalized girls in India, which would be delivered by a local nonprofit and, if successful, paid for by a Western aid budget. Payments to investors would be based on two measures: the girls' enrollment in school and their learning improvement. A control group of girls taking the same standardized tests in other schools would provide the benchmark for gauging the success of the program. Other development-impact bonds now under consideration include programs to eliminate sleeping sickness in Uganda and to cut HIV infection rates in Swaziland.

A SIB structure may not even require any public money at all. A pilot program in Fresno, California, has been testing the potential for a SIB variant called a health-impact bond. Fresno is home to around two hundred thousand individuals who suffer from asthma; the pilot is targeting a group of two hundred children in the county, who average 1.5 emergency-room visits a year. By funding a variety of simple preventative measures in the children's homes, like cleaning and replacing carpets, Collective Health, the nonprofit organization behind the pilot, is hoping to demonstrate substantial savings to health insurers. If it can do so, the next step would be to launch a full SIB in which insurance firms would fund payments to investors out of savings reaped from fewer claims.

WHAT ABOUT THE other two parties to the transaction beside the SIB commissioner? The obvious benefit to the organization doing the actual work is that a SIB keeps the funding flowing. As the amount of government money shrinks, charities need to find other ways to raise funds. Social providers also have their feet held to the fire, as performance is measured against payment triggers. Those data can provide precious new insights. In Peterborough data dashboards show everything from how being met at the prison gates affects reoffending rates to month-by-month comparisons of caseworkers' activities.

That sounds horribly corporate to many: how can something intangible like reintegrating people into society be reduced to a set of numbers? But without such numbers, how can anyone know what works? Without the incentive to review learning outcomes, for example, an educational project for Indian schoolgirls might blindly allocate the same amount of time to each child in the program. With that information in mind, however, the data might prompt teachers to spend three hours with a child who needs more attention and only one with another who doesn't.

In some ways, too, private sources of funding can be less brutal than government ones. SIBs are designed to be a more patient form of capital. Government contracts tend to run on cycles of twelve to twenty-four months, but the toughest social problems are never going to be solved in that sort of time frame. Investors are prepared to lock their money up for longer: the Peterborough SIB was initially designed to run for a six-year period, for example. That means providers can plan and staff up with certainty. They also have freedom to experiment. The people helped by SIBs are often chaotic. Ex-prisoners tend not to be organized and methodical, for example; many have addictions or suffer from conditions such as depression. Clients often drift in and out of contact. That means it is vital to be flexible in the way that the service is run. Martinez Sutherland, the habitual offender in Peterborough, had been running very short of money in the run-up to Christmas 2013, for example. One Service eased the strain, and any temptation to stray, by giving him £25 of lunch vouchers.

Such flexibility offers the potential for something very elusive in the world of social enterprise: the chance to "scale up." The promise of a successful financial system is that capital gets allocated to where it can be most productively employed. A private start-up has a range of options to tap capital as it moves from its very earliest days (angel investing or, as we shall see in a later chapter, crowd-funding) to a road-tested business (venture capital and bank lending) to an established commercial enterprise (private equity, banks, and capital markets). If a for-profit business does well, it can raise money to get bigger.

Nonprofits find it much harder to get hold of the money that would enable them to grow. Between 1970 and 2007, more than 200,000 nonprofits opened in the United States, but only 144 of them reached $50 million in annual revenue. Why should this be? Governments are bound by short budgeting timetables, by procurement requirements, by shifting political winds, and by a fear of funding failures—and now by a shortfall of money. They are an unreliable source of capital. The purely philanthropic model of funding suffers from similar unpredictability. Philanthropists will often commit money for a period of two to three years and then stop. Sir Ronald himself used to follow this model in his own giving: without any way of measuring the outcome of his donations, the only leverage he had was to cut off funding. But as he started to examine social investment, he realized that this pattern constrained people even as it funded them. It is very difficult for social enterprises to think about ramping up when the funding is liable suddenly to dry up. But if organizations can demonstrate a record of success that delivers both good social outcomes and commercial returns, then the money is likely to keep on coming.[6]

LET'S SPIN THE ISSUE around to look at SIBs from the investors' perspective. For philanthropists, the social-impact bond enables greater rigor in how they deploy their money. Rather than handing cash over to a provider and hoping for the best, the investor gets data on how things are going over the life of a project. Even an unsuccessful SIB program has value, by giving investors information with which to sift future giving opportunities.

The London homelessness bond, for example, tracks metrics in five categories in total: the number of people in the target group who are still rough sleeping; placements into accommodation; efforts to reconnect rough sleepers with their families; health issues, including emergency-room visits; and progress into work. Payments started being made to investors within a few months of the program's launch. The setup, as Sir Ronald would recognize, is not dissimilar to the reports that private-equity investors receive on the firms owned by their funds.

But the idea behind social-impact bonds, and behind impact investing in general, is not just that this is a better way of measuring outcomes. It is also that financial returns will increase the overall amount of capital available for social programs. The hard question is how far along the continuum of financial returns should you go to attract more of this capital?

The Peterborough SIB is typical of a first crack at a financial innovation. It asks investors to take on a lot of risk in order to test the product. If the recidivism rate improves by 7 percent, say, it will nonetheless fall below the target specified in the Peterborough contract, and the investors will lose all their cash. It may be called a social-impact "bond," but it functions much more like risk-taking equity capital.

That bargain might work for a bunch of committed charitable foundations and philanthropic individuals. One of the investors in the homelessness bond in London is a wealthy individual whose son has spent time living rough, for example, so he has deeply personal reasons to fund the work. But it's too much risk to attract big pools of capital. On the other hand, if the returns on offer to investors were much higher to compensate for that risk, then they would start to outweigh the savings that government makes from lower crime rates.

So in a pattern that is typical of early-stage financial innovation, each SIB is a slightly different variant on the last, as participants experiment with different balances between social and financial outcomes. The New York City prisoner-rehabilitation program protects a chunk of Goldman's investment: a guarantee from Bloomberg Philanthropies, the former mayor's foundation, caps the amount of money the bank can lose if recidivism targets are not met. Some think this model—in which philanthropists, or perhaps government itself, guarantee that a portion of investors' money is returned—is the way to bring in more capital.

Another option is to blend the returns from SIBs with other assets. Allia, a British charity devoted to social investment, made a SIB available to retail investors for the first time in 2013. It made the risk acceptable with a simple bit of financial engineering. Of every £1,000 invested in the Allia bond, £780 goes to a fixed-rate loan to a social-housing provider, which when repaid with interest will give investors their £1,000 back. Another £200 goes into the SIB providing multisystemic therapy to troubled children in Essex, which offers investors the potential for an additional return. (Fees eat up the other £20.) The structure is not risk free: investors are exposed to the risk of the housing provider going bust. But they are not dependent on the performance of the SIB to get their (nominal) principal back.

These variants all try to blunt the risks being taken by investors. That should increase the pot of money that could be attracted. Sir Ronald Cohen's philosophy as a venture capitalist was to look for "the second bounce of the ball," anticipating the next step in an industry. He thinks the natural evolution of the social-investment market is for charitable foundations and trusts to allocate a proportion of their money to SIBs and other types of social-financing instruments, in effect turning them into an asset class.

Others think there is a big opportunity to attract individual givers. People are very generous with their cash. In a typical year, total gifts of money (as opposed to time spent volunteering) for charitable purposes in the United States exceed 2 percent of GDP. According to John List, an economist at the University of Chicago, giving has grown at double the growth rate of the S&P 500 since 1968. Individual givers are the most lavish with their money, accounting for 75 percent of total American giving annually.[7]

If people are prepared to give to charity in the knowledge that they will not see the money again, how much more might they put aside if there was a reasonable prospect of getting some cash back? The answer depends on why people give in the first place. One theory emphasizes the benefits that accrue to recipients: the purpose of giving is to achieve an outcome, whether that is having fewer homeless people on the street or lower rates of recidivism. For these sorts of genuinely altruistic givers, the idea of outcomes-based funding ought to be highly attractive. Donations are more effective; as money comes back to investors, it can be plowed back into other charitable activities.

There is another theory of charitable giving, however. Known as "impure altruism," it emphasizes the benefits that accrue to a donor: the warm glow that results from giving or the improved image of the donor in the eyes of others. If people give to feel and look saintly, then monetary incentives of the sort that social-impact bonds dangle may actually do more harm than good. Angels aren't supposed to get paid, after all. Getting a financial return muddies the signal that giving is meant to be sending.

That idea has been around since at least 1970, when Richard Titmuss, a British social scientist, hypothesized that paying for blood donations would actually have the effect of reducing the amount of blood that is given. A recent piece of research looked at this concern. Participants in an experiment were asked to donate to the American Red Cross by clicking a pair of keys on a keyboard in turn for a period of up to five minutes. The experiment was designed to reveal the extent of participants' motivation: each pair of clicks resulted in a donation to the charity, although the amount given gradually declined the more times people clicked. You had to be motivated to keep clicking all the way through the allocated time. Some participants were told they would have to make their donations public, and others donated privately; some were given payments, while others were not. The results showed that when there were no payments involved, the people whose donations were public made significantly more effort than those whose efforts remained confidential. Altruism does seem to be impure: recognition matters.[8]

When payments were factored in, a different picture emerged. For participants whose results were made public, there was a slight decline in output when there was money to be made. This was the effect Titmuss predicted. But private donors put a lot more effort in when there was a financial incentive than when there wasn't. All of which suggests that offering a financial reward can be unhelpful when people want to advertise their goodness, but potentially very attractive in unlocking pools of capital for social enterprises when people make private decisions.

BY NOW SOME READERS will be feeling distinctly queasy. There is something suspicious about introducing the idea of financial incentives into state-funded social programs, let alone charitable funding. If Goldman Sachs and prisons are going to be mentioned in the same sentence, many think it ought to be for different reasons than a social-impact bond. Anders Lustgarten, a playwright, has already made social-impact bonds the villain of *If You Don't Let Us Dream, We Won't Let You Sleep*, a play that ran in London's West End in early 2013. The play featured a thinly disguised variant of SIBs called "Unity bonds," which become targets for speculators who position themselves to make money from rises in things like homelessness and drug addiction.

Such dystopianism cannot simply be dismissed. Some public services are indispensable: they cannot be contingent on finding private investors or on the realization of cashable savings. Financial incentives are prone to lead to distortions: it is possible to imagine social enterprises concentrating on relatively easier cases in order to deliver better outcomes or even keeping at-risk children who do need to be in the care of the state with their families in order to meet targets. That is why it is so important to have clean data and independent monitoring of SIB programs.

But any disquiet is also wildly premature. The second chapter of this book showed how trouble starts to brew when mainstream finance picks up a product and runs with it. SIBs are right at the start of their life. Getting markets off the ground takes time: instruments have to become standardized, markets have to deepen, an entire infrastructure of contracts, prices, and participants has to develop. Sir

Ronald had to beaver away for ten years before the first social-impact bond was launched. Each instrument that has followed has been the fruit of slow negotiations between investors, providers, commissioners, and intermediaries. They have taken months to put together. In the jargon, they suffer from high transaction costs.

And getting from where SIBs are now to a wider implementation depends on a lot of things going right. The availability of capital at scale is unproven. Investors in Peterborough have been willing to take more risk than many others would. And plans can easily be disrupted by changes in policy. In April 2014, for example, the Conservative government announced that the last cohort of prisoners that had been due to join the Peterborough SIB would be enrolled instead into a new nationwide probation policy that would seek to build on the lessons learned in the Peterborough experiment.

Worrying about where SIBs might lead also requires you to think about the counterfactual: if not this type of funding, then which? The state has not been good at innovating to solve big social problems. The indispensable elements of public-service provision—health-care services, above all—are gobbling up ever more money, squeezing funding for discretionary prevention-based programs. Social-impact bonds will never be the only answer to the problem of the shrinking state. But they are an extremely promising avenue to explore. Just ask Martinez Sutherland, the ex-prisoner in Peterborough, who by the summer of 2014 had turned his initial work placement into a full-time job at a builders' merchant. He was in work, in accommodation, paying his own bills, and keen to give One Service credit for the turnaround. He may not have cared much how the program was funded, but his life had improved because of a dose of financial creativity.

CHAPTER 5

LIVE LONG AND PROSPER

The Sloan School of Management at the Massachusetts Institute of Technology is housed in a swish new building in Boston. The neat lawns and quiet, carpeted corridors may seem far removed from the bustle and brashness of Wall Street, but as we saw in the opening chapter, the worlds of finance and theory have long been intertwined. Such linkages have deepened in the past forty years. Mathematicians pore over the models that price derivatives and manage risks. Quants program the algorithms that power ultrafast trading strategies. In the years after the 2007–2008 crisis, regulators have become increasingly interested in what disciplines like epidemiology and ecology have to say about the stability and interconnectedness of financial networks. The preoccupations of the MIT finance faculty may start off as blips on the edge of the radar of the mainstream industry—but they have a habit of moving inward.

For Andrew Lo and Robert Merton, two of the academics on the building's sixth floor, their concerns are literally matters of life and death. Lo, a genial fifty-something, thinks finance can increase our chances of surviving killer diseases. Merton, a Nobel Prize–winning economist and one of the men behind the equation that launched the age of derivatives, believes it can help ensure that re-tirees enjoy the fruits of higher longevity. One wants to take on cancer, the other the misery of penurious old age. Neither is blind to the flaws of finance, but both are firm believers in its power to solve real-world problems.

Lo's goal is to improve the economics of drug research. The semiconductor industry has Moore's law, a rule of thumb that states that computer chips double in power every eighteen months or so. The pharmaceutical industry suffers from the reverse. Eroom's law is the ironic name for a troubling trend: the number of new drugs approved by the US Food and Drug Administration for every bil-lion dollars spent on R&D halves roughly every nine years. A slow-down in medical breakthroughs matters to everyone. Estimates suggest that three-quarters of the improvements in life expectancy realized between 2000 and 2009 can be attributed to pharmaceuti-cal innovation.[1]

The reasons for Eroom's law are complicated: stricter regulatory scrutiny of new drugs plays a part, as does the fact that it gets harder to improve on existing products. But the upshot is simple: investors are losing interest in an industry that delivers less bang for their bucks. The share prices of listed pharmaceutical companies have been languishing. The number of venture-capital firms active in the biotechnology industry has declined. The financing shortfall is par-ticularly acute in the phase of drug development that bridges basic research and clinical trials of a new medicine. This "translational" period, which moves a promising piece of academic research into the early stages of testing for use in humans, is known to the industry as "the valley of death." It is this part of the drug-discovery process, when risks are highest and capital is scarcest, that Andrew Lo wants to address. His goal is to unlock billions of dollars of funding for early-stage drugs. And to drum up interest, he and others have formulated a provocative question: "Can financial engineering cure cancer?"[2]

Lo is not an ivory-tower zealot. Well before the financial crisis, he was struck by the failure of the "efficient-market hypothesis" to grapple with the basics of human behavior. The essence of the efficient-markets hypothesis, which was formulated in 1970 by a University of Chicago economist named Eugene Fama, who shared the 2013 Nobel Prize for Economics, is that markets are rational. The hypothesis posits that market prices incorporate all the publicly available information on a given security and that people respond rationally to this information. The desire to make simplifying assumptions is understandable in finance—"Can you imagine how hard physics would be if electrons had feelings?" is the question Richard Feynman, a physicist, once asked—but this one takes the cake. Humans are not always rational, and markets are swayed by sentiment as much as logic. Instead of the efficient-market hypothesis, Lo champions something called the "adaptive-market hypothesis," which takes the world as it is rather than as it should be.

The AMH accepts that some market behavior is hardwired. Our brains have been programmed by evolution to respond to emotions such as fear and greed. Financial markets are the perfect playground for these emotions, a theater that is dedicated to volatility and risk, to losing and winning. In one study of which parts of the brain become active in response to monetary rewards, volunteers were given a fifty-dollar opening stake and then shown a series of animated wheel-of-fortune spinners that either added to their cash or subtracted from it. As the rewards piled up, researchers saw activity in the parts of the brain that release a chemical called dopamine, a neurotransmitter triggered by pleasurable activities. Something about these patterns of activity looked very familiar to the researchers. Then they noticed that the images they were looking at mimicked those displayed by cocaine addicts and first-time morphine users. The brain appears to respond to monetary gains and addictive drugs in the same way.[3]

As with greed, so with fear. In his entertaining book on the physiology of trading, John Coates, a trader turned neuroscientist, examines the effects of testosterone and cortisol on risk appetite and aversion. One of his experiments, on the employees of a London trading floor, showed that cortisol levels in traders' saliva jump by as much as 500 percent in a day. Cortisol is a hormone produced in response to stress: Coates found that increases in its levels were directly correlated to a financial-market measure called "implied volatility," which functions as a gauge of uncertainty. And these, remember, are the professionals.[4]

All of which suggests that the logical, efficient part of our brain is not always in charge. It is extremely hard to stick to an optimal portfolio allocation when the world is going to hell. When volatility spikes, fear rises. People panic, sell assets they regard as risky, and rush for safer ones, like government bonds and cash. Lo's answer to this behavior has been to set up funds designed to protect investors by setting a kind of cruise-control mechanism. When volatility starts to rise, the funds automatically reduce their holdings of stocks; when volatility becomes more subdued, the funds start to take their equity exposures up again. The funds do what investors instinctively want, in other words, but they do so smoothly, not in violent lurches.

This kind of thinking puts Lo at an interesting crossroads, suspicious of finance's capacity to run riot but convinced of its ability to do good. To cross the valley of death in drug research, he proposes to create a drug-development "megafund" that would raise up to $30 billion to invest in promising anticancer drugs by using one of the most suspected techniques in financial engineering.

That technique is "securitization," a word that is now commonly understood to mean blowing up the world's financial system but is more properly described as a way of bringing together fragmented cash flows—the mortgages and credit-card payments of many individuals, say—into a single income stream. The prospect of repayments from this income stream can be used to raise capital from investors, just as a company can raise capital by issuing a bond that will be repaid from its future earnings. Securitization has a terrible reputation because of the performance of mortgage-backed securities during the crisis, but its underlying logic is sound.

In particular, securitization reduces risk by diversifying investors' bets. As we have seen in the first chapter, the advantages of diversification have long been known—to Chinese merchants thousands of years ago and to Geneva bankers in the eighteenth century. But it was first captured in formal theory in 1952, when a twenty-five-year-old graduate student at the University of Chicago named Harry

Markowitz published a paper called "Portfolio Selection." The gist of Markowitz's theory was that the return on an investment had to be weighed against the risk of its going awry and that these "risk-adjusted" returns could be improved by diversifying. Putting all your money into the shares of a single firm might deliver a high return, but it exposes you to disaster if that firm goes broke. Better to spread your money across different bets, be they geographies, industries, or asset classes. Securitization is another take on this idea: by pulling a lot of different loans into a single investable security, the income stream it produces should become more stable.

Lo's idea for a drug-development megafund uses the same logic. The drugs would be at different stages of development, from later-stage projects that are already throwing off royalties to early-stage ones that have yet to come to market. Some technologies may not even have been developed yet: one option would be to give the best people at a lot of different research hospitals a funding stream in return for getting 10 percent of whatever comes out of the labs. The combined cash flows from these assets would go to investors. If the fund had a large enough portfolio of drugs, Lo reckons, some of them would be pretty sure of commercial success.

Reactions to the megafund concept, which was first floated in a paper in *Nature Biotechnology* in 2012, have been positive. Lo and his colleagues have released a follow-up paper answering a stream of questions; investment bankers, never slow to sniff a moneymaking opportunity, attended a packed seminar on the megafund idea that was held in 2013. Raising a multibillion-dollar fund is going to take a long time, but Lo is hopeful that a smaller proof-of-concept fund, devoted to drugs for "orphan" diseases that affect fewer than two hundred thousand individuals, will come to fruition more quickly.

Some people will be holding their heads in their hands at the thought of using securitization to take on cancer. Isn't this the same sort of financial wizardry that created those infamous collateralized-debt obligations that were stuffed with subprime loans during the mortgage boom? In an echo of these instruments, Lo and his colleagues have christened the proposed drug megafund "research-backed obligations." Why invest hope in a technology that caused so much damage? For that matter, why aim for such a big amount? Couldn't Lo make life easier for himself and aim for a smaller, simpler fund?

The answer to that question tells you something about why financial engineering exists at all. First, the funds need to be so big because it is only by diversifying their investments across a lot of different assets that investors can be reasonably sure that enough will succeed to generate the required returns. The earlier in the development process a drug is, the greater the amount of uncertainty attached to it. And the greater the amount of uncertainty, the more important it is to spread your bets. This is also an argument for having a megafund devoted to a lot of different diseases, rather than one focused on cancer. But that would bring costs of its own by making it harder for investors to assess the portfolio. And since cancer is itself a collection of many different diseases, with a lot of different potential treatments, there is already plenty of scope for diversification.

If diversification is the key to providing a more acceptable mix of risk and reward, then Lo's proposed megafund needs to hold a lot of assets. The more assets, the more shots on goal, is the way he puts it. That in turn means the funds must be able to attract a lot of capital to fund these assets. And that means they need to be able to attract investors in debt instruments like bonds. Far more money flows each year to bonds than shares. The amount of corporate debt issued in the United States in 2013 was almost $1.4 trillion; the amount of equity raised through initial public offerings (IPOs) did not even top $100 billion.[5]

This difference in heft partly reflects the fact that investors regard it as a safer investment than equity. Shareholders are at the back of the line for payments from the companies they own and at the front of it for losses when a firm goes bust. Bondholders are at the front of the line for payments, including when a company enters bankruptcy. If you are a conservative investor, you prefer debt.[6]

To draw debt investors into a fund made up of a lot of risky assets, diversification provides a measure of reassurance. But it is not enough for the most cautious. So securitization has some other features designed to make them feel safer. In particular, Lo proposes to use the structuring techniques of securitization to create different classes of investor within the fund. The cash flows that the fund assets generate will go first to the most senior debt holders, then to investors in lower debt tranches, and finally to equity investors. If things go wrong, the most senior debt investors will have first claim on the assets inside the fund. The protection of being higher up the capital structure than others has another effect: it makes it more likely that the most senior tranches can gain a credit rating.

Ratings are not just an important source of third-party analysis for investors, particularly smaller ones that don't have the resources to conduct detailed assessments of every issuer's financial health. They are also part of the skeleton of the financial system. After the 1930s (a decade now lauded for its postcrisis regulatory overhaul), US banks were required by their regulators to use credit ratings to assess the creditworthiness of the fixed-income instruments they invest in; international rules still use ratings to determine the amount of equity banks have to use to fund these assets. Investment firms use credit ratings to specify what types of fixed-income products they can invest in, and the biggest pools of capital—pension funds, sovereign-wealth funds, and the like—are often confined to "investment-grade securities," which carry a higher rating. You can see why Andrew Lo wants to do whatever he can to win over the ratings agencies: they open the door to the largest amounts of money.

To add another level of protection, Lo also thinks there might be room for a third party to come in and offer a guarantee, so that if the drugs in the megafund fail to deliver enough income, the guarantor will make up the shortfall. That might be a suitable role for nonprofit organizations and charitable foundations, which could use the promise of a guarantee as a lever to attract a lot of private capital. But the trouble with guarantees is that they work only if they are credible, which means they have to be extended by someone in—or, more precisely, perceived to be in—a rock-solid financial position. And the trouble with rock-solid guarantees, as Lo himself acknowledges, is that they can dampen the incentives on the part of investors to do their own homework on the risks they are taking.

Lo is a long way from having to worry about that. The cancer megafund is an idea at the start of its life rather than one that has been thrashed to within an inch of it. Asset classes have to get very big before they can have an impact on the financial system as a whole, let alone potentially require the taxpayer to step in when things go wrong. And even if you do fret about speculative excess, he says, better that investors' animal spirits are directed toward solving the biggest social issues than to funding the purchase of McMansions. But he is alive to the potential dangers of securitization.

For example, the benefits of diversification come about only if assets in the fund genuinely do not all rise and fall together—in the jargon, if they are "noncorrelated." Putting your money into a basket of equities spreads your risk across a lot of different companies, but that isn't much help if the whole stock market tanks; investing in mortgages across the United States is all very well unless there is a national downturn. "If we learned one thing from the crisis," says Lo, "it is that correlations matter."

That has implications for which diseases can support a fund. Lo's plan for a smaller proof-of-concept fund focuses on orphan diseases for a reason. These illnesses are often too rare to be interesting to investors on their own, but put enough of them together and attitudes might change. What's more, because orphan diseases reflect separate, random mutations of genes, there is less likelihood of correlation between them: if one drug fails, it does not mean that the chances of a cure for other diseases go down. Lo is less hopeful about the prospects of a megafund for Alzheimer's disease, however. Since the science in tackling this disease is at an early stage, there are just too few decent projects in existence to ensure enough diversification.

Lo is also clear about the importance of proper due diligence. Investors in the megafunds will need to analyze all the risks properly—from correlation to the statistical likelihood of success for each asset in the fund. Making things safer is fine—indeed, it is part of the way that markets reach real scale. But as the sedating effects of the AAA credit rating showed during the mortgage crisis, lulling people into a state of complacency is not.

As Lo DESCRIBES his megafund idea to me, a head pokes around the door to ask if he wants to grab some lunch. The head belongs to Robert Merton, one of the people who enabled the derivatives market to explode and a former director of Long-Term Capital Management, the hedge fund whose geniuses failed in 1998. But when you meet Merton, the thing that comes across most strongly is that he is a car nut.

His conversation is peppered with analogies from the automobile industry. Discussing the adjustable-rate mortgage, whose interest rate jumps up and down and exposes home owners to the risk of sudden leaps in their payments, he compares it to "General Motors developing the one-door car because it suits the car firm." Talking about the moves that have been made to make banks safer, he worries that people tend to drive four-wheel-drive vehicles faster because they have the comfort of additional safety.

The automotive industry was where the young Merton intended to make his career; he studied engineering at Columbia University. But economics and finance were to claim him. Merton's name was made in the 1970s, with work that paralleled research by two older academics, Fischer Black and Myron Scholes. Together the three men cracked the problem of how to price an option, a financial instrument that gives the buyer the right, but not the obligation, to buy or sell an underlying asset.

The question of what price to pay for an option was one to which there was no rigorous answer until Black, Scholes, and Merton came along. The answer they came up with, expressed as what is now known as the Black-Scholes equation, was based on the idea that the price of the option ought to be the same as the cost of constructing a perfect hedge for the underlying asset. The Black-Scholes formula, which coincided with the computerization of trading, enabled the rapid pricing of options and paved the way for huge growth in derivatives markets.[7]

At a time when *financial innovation* and *derivatives* have become dirty words, Merton has become practiced at answering the criticisms thrown their way. "When you get asked, 'What is it like to be an ax murderer?' you tend to question the premise" is how he puts it. The fact that credit-default swaps, a type of insurance against default, caused so much trouble during the crisis? "Oh, boy, what a surprise," he says. "We had a credit crisis, so CDS was bound to be the one that got into trouble. It's like saying a property insurer got into trouble after Sandy [the superstorm that hit New York and other Eastern Seaboard cities in 2012]."

The problem that most preoccupies Merton now picks up where Andrew Lo's megafund idea leaves off. Whereas Lo wants to increase people's chances of living *longer,* Merton wants to increase their chances of living longer *well.* Of all the problems faced by the rich world, human longevity can claim to be the biggest. Between 1960 and 2010, life expectancy at the age of 65 in rich countries rose by about 4 years for men and by more than 5 for women. To-day's 65-year-old Americans can expect to live 19.2 more years, up from 16.4 years in 1980. That might not sound like a massive change, but the effects are enormous because of the changing structure of the population in rich countries. In the United States, the great wave of baby boomers, the postwar generation born between 1946 and 1964, is now entering its gardening years. The US Census Bureau estimates the number of baby boomers at 78.2 million; they are now retiring at a rate of 10,000 people a day.[8]

From a low base, the ranks of the very old are growing the fastest. Actuaries like to talk about "rectangularization" to describe the changing demography of societies. The term refers to the shape of the curve on a chart that shows what proportion of a population born in a certain year remains alive after a certain age. If the age of people's deaths was evenly spaced, the line would be a downward-sloping diagonal. As more of us live to a ripe old age before dying, the line becomes more rectangular. Figure 2, which shows the changing life curves of the British population since 1851, illustrates the phenomenon. Half of Britons born in 1851 were dead in their mid-40s, and only a quarter saw their 70th birthdays; by contrast, 84 percent of those born in 2011 are projected to reach the age of 70.

More old people means more spending—on pensions, on social care, and on health care. In a 2012 analysis, the International Monetary Fund (IMF) tried to put some numbers on the pension costs of aging populations. The fund used the idea of a "replacement rate," the percentage of a pensioner's preretirement income that enables them to keep the same standard of living. If you allow for the benefit of lower taxes and a reduced need to save, then pensioners

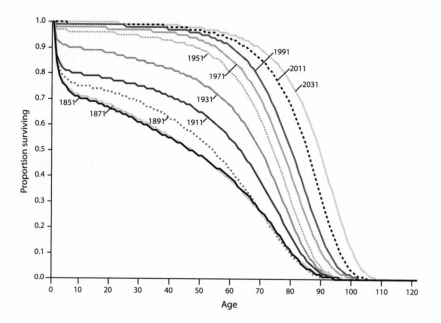

Proportion of people in England and Wales, by year of birth, alive at each age (based on actual or projected mortality rates). *Source: UK Office for National Statistics*

can probably get by on 60–80 percent of their working income. By assuming a 60 percent replacement rate and using United Nations projections for increases in life expectancy between 2010 and 2050, the IMF reckons that the aggregate pension costs of the elderly will roughly double in that period. Over the full forty-year period, the cost of aging is put at an additional 100 percent of 2010 GDP for rich economies and about half that amount in emerging economies. And this number is for pension costs only; it does not include the costs of long-term care and health care.[9]

These gloomy estimates are based on current projections for improvements in life expectancy. But what if people live longer than expected? That would not be surprising. The track record of actuarial forecasts is one of consistent underestimation: a survey of twenty-year projections of longevity in the United States, Australia, Canada, Japan, and New Zealand found that they tended to be too low by an average of three years. For individuals, those extra years are cause for celebration; for society, they mean the bill for aging goes higher still. Insurers who are funding annuities must pay out for longer; so too must defined-benefit pension schemes, which require employers to pay retired employees a fixed proportion of their final salary for as long as they live. The IMF's 2012 analysis estimated the effects of this "longevity risk." If everyone lived three years longer than now expected, the costs of pensions alone could increase by (yet) another 50 percent of GDP by 2050.

The burden of looking after the elderly has conventionally been financed by the current generation of taxpayers, which is fine when there are enough young people to pay out. The problem is that the population pyramid is gradually being inverted as fertility rates drop. Demographers use the term *peak child* to describe their expectation that the number of children born per year globally has reached its zenith. In 1950 children (15-year-olds and under) accounted for 27 percent of the developed world's total population and the over-60s for only 12 percent. By 2013 the proportions had pretty much reversed—older people accounted for 23 percent of the population and children for 16 percent. The upshot is that there are fewer young people to support more elderly folk. In rich-world countries in 1950, there were 7.2 people aged 20–64 for every person aged 65 and over. That ratio had fallen to 4.1 to 1 by the start of this decade, and by 2050 the burden of supporting each pensioner will fall on 2 people.[10]

Put all these numbers together, and they don't add up. People are living longer. Populations are aging. The costs of providing for retirees' golden years are soaring, and there are not enough younger people coming up behind to support the burden.

Policy makers are already gingerly making changes to address this problem. One obvious option is to keep people working for longer. The retirement age is edging up in country after country: increases are under way or planned in most of the thirty-four countries of the Organization for Economic Co-operation and Development (OECD). But the changes to date are insufficient. The hikes in retirement ages are expected to keep pace with improved life expectancy only in six OECD countries for men and in ten countries for women. Only a handful of countries, such as Denmark and Italy, formally link retirement ages to changes in life expectancy.[11]

Governments are also becoming less generous in the benefits they offer, putting more emphasis on private pensions. At the same time, the private-pension offering is being squeezed. The defined-benefit or final-salary scheme is disappearing, as employers balk at an obligation that in some cases dwarfs the actual business. The future of private-pension provision is the defined-contribution scheme, in which the employer and the individual worker put money into a pension pot, and the individual makes do with whatever amount they eventually get out.

The DC market is particularly well developed in the United States. The problem is that the amount of money people are saving is still insufficient. Social Security (America's federal government pension system) provides a replacement rate of about 35 percent of a typical family's income, but that still leaves a large gap to fill. The average American household has virtually nothing set aside for that purpose. One 2013 analysis reckoned that the median amount of retirement savings was three thousand dollars for all working-age households (that is, not just those with retirement accounts) and twelve thousand dollars for those near retirement. That pays for a blowout vacation, not decades of old age.[12]

Opinions differ on when exactly the full scale of the shortfall in pension pots will come home to roost. For some cities, like Detroit, where a shrinking population meant a shrinking tax base with which to fund benefits, it has already become clear that the economics do not work. But in general, this is not a cliff-like problem, where people suddenly run out of money. The money that households have saved will last them for a while, particularly if they can put off retirement by working longer (an option that will be more available to educated workers). "It will become a big issue when parents find their standard of living is going down and their children see it too," predicts Alicia Munnell of the Center for Retirement Research at Boston College.

As the defined-benefit schemes fade and people grasp the extent of the shortfalls in their own defined-contribution pots, Merton thinks he will find more takers for a brainchild of his called SmartNest. This is a retirement-planning tool that Merton designed and subsequently sold to an asset manager called Dimensional Fund Advisors in 2009. SmartNest is available to members of firms' DC schemes and uses everything from behavioral nudges to complicated hedging techniques to try to deliver a decent standard of living at retirement. His starting point is based on the idea of the replacement rate. SmartNest calculates the percentage of pensioners' preretirement income that enables them to keep the same standard of living for the rest of their lives, without having to worry about the effect of inflation. Because the product is designed to deliver a flow of income, rather than a pot of money, its aim is to ensure that a person has enough cash upon retirement to be able to buy an annuity that produces the desired stream of cash.

When the product calculates that a person is falling short of his or her desired retirement income, it doesn't give the person the option to start making decisions on what assets to invest in. Making a decision about whether to put money into equities or bonds is not something that most people feel qualified to do, and in any case it is only a means to an end. "It's the same as understanding how a car engine works," says Merton, returning to his beloved cars. "It is important, but it is not meaningful to most drivers."

Instead, users have three less technical levers to pull. They can save more by diverting more of their monthly salary to savings. They can change their assumed retirement date and work longer. Or they can change the minimum level of income they can retire on—below the amount of money they need to maintain their working-life standard of living but still enough to live on. SmartNest adds up the income streams that people can already count on, like Social Security payments and any accrued defined-benefit pension entitlements, and holds a really conservative portfolio of assets—things like government bonds—to achieve an assured minimum. The higher the minimum level of income that a person specifies, the more of their savings get put into these conservative assets and the less of it goes into riskier assets, like equities, that have the potential to deliver higher income. Raising the minimum threshold means that investment allocations are altered behind the scenes: more conservative assets, fewer risky ones. So if a SmartNest saver is off-track to meet the desired income level upon retirement, he also has the option of dropping the minimum-income target. These three choices have the benefit of spelling out the stark logic of the pension squeeze: save more, work longer, or take more risks.

All the time SmartNest is hard at work under the hood crunching all sorts of numbers, from an individual's stream of future pension contributions to the assumed returns on a portfolio of assets, to come up with its assessment of likely retirement income. It also uses more complicated techniques to hedge an employee's risks. Inflation-protected Treasury bills guard against any drops below the minimum-income target. By selling call options on stocks in the portfolio, which give the buyer the right to buy the equities in question at an agreed price, the plan gives up the chance of shoot-the-lights-out returns in exchange for a nice pot of cash. In effect, Merton is using financial engineering to turn defined-contribution schemes into something that looks more like a defined-benefit scheme, where the returns neither dip below a minimum income target nor exceed the desired level.

MERTON'S BRAINCHILD is interesting not just because it is an attempt to address a huge social problem using some of the derivatives that are now widely demonized. He is very deliberately trying to work with the grain of human behavior rather than against it. Merton describes the product as being a bit like a regular physical examination, in which working-age savers are sent alerts telling them how far off their desired income goal they are. It is a conscious effort to cater to ordinary people, those folks who never become seriously engaged in the process of planning for retirement and who need to be given choices that have a meaning. Other firms are also adopting the use of simple devices to focus people's minds on how much income they can expect to receive. BlackRock has launched an index called CoRI, which is meant to give fifty-five- to sixty-four-year-olds an instant estimate of how much retirement income their current level of savings would provide.

In this emphasis on how people actually think about their finances, Merton echoes the stance of Andrew Lo. The 2007–2008 crisis has given a big shove to the school of thinking known as "behavioral finance." Behavioral finance is designed to exploit the gap between two types of human. One is *Homo economicus,* an idealized character whose choices are driven entirely by rational calculation and who inhabits academic models. The other is *Homo sapiens,* a more familiar species whose decision making is less rational and who lives in the real world. In no area of life is the distance between these two individuals greater than the world of money, and in no part of the financial landscape is the gap wider than saving for retirement.

Homo economicus would start saving for retirement as early as possible, putting aside money in order for the magic of "compound interest" to do its stuff. A forty-year-old saving ten thousand dollars a year will accumulate seven hundred thousand dollars by the time he is seventy, assuming an average annual interest rate of 5 percent. To get to the same pot from a starting age of thirty, he would need to save only fifty-five hundred dollars a year.

Homo sapiens, by contrast, finds the subject of pensions baffling and dull. Only 46 percent of Americans report that they or their spouse have tried to calculate how much money they will need to have saved by the time they stop working so that they can live comfortably in retirement. The propensity of people to plan for retirement is heavily influenced by personal circumstances rather than dispassionate analysis. If you have an older sibling, you are more likely to plan for retirement; if your older brother or sister is in a worse financial situation than you are, the likelihood increases further. People whose parents suffered health problems or lived in nursing homes before dying are more likely to think about retirement.[13]

The temptation to put things off is snappily known to economists as "hyperbolic discounting." The basic idea is that people's short-term actions are inconsistent with their long-term aims. When it comes to eating more healthily or giving up smoking or looking for a more fulfilling job, the "future you" is clear-eyed about what is desirable. But the "current you" does not want the future to arrive.

In an old but delicious study into hyperbolic discounting that is almost guaranteed to bring about a burst of self-recognition, researchers gave people a choice of films to rent. The list of titles was divided into highbrow films like *Blue, Raise the Red Lantern,* and *The Piano* and lowbrow films like *Groundhog Day, The Mask,* and *So I Married an Axe Murderer.* Participants had to choose titles to rent for that night and for two other nights further in the future. Inevitably, the most distant of the three dates had the highest proportion of highbrow films; the lowbrow films were far more popular when they were going to be watched that night. You know you ought to watch *Lincoln,* but when push comes to shove, you end up in front of *Paul Blart: Mall Cop.* It's the same story with pensions. Everyone knows they ought to be saving, but when the time comes, the value you place on spending today versus putting money aside for tomorrow shifts toward vice and away from virtue.[14]

Adding to this behavioral problem is another one: financial illiteracy. Since 1992, at intervals of every two years, the University of Michigan Health and Retirement Study has surveyed a representative sample of more than twenty-six thousand Americans over the age of fifty. Among the questions it poses are the following three deliberately simple questions:[15]

- Suppose you had $100 in a savings account and the interest rate was 2 percent per year. After five years, how much do you think you would have in the account if you left the money to grow: more than $102, exactly $102, less than $102?

- Imagine that the interest rate on your savings account was 1 percent per year and inflation was 2 percent per year. After one year, would you be able to buy more than, exactly the same as, or less than today with the money in this account?

- Do you think that the following statement is true or false? "Buying a single company stock usually provides a safer return than a stock mutual fund."

Two-thirds of respondents get the first question, on compound interest, right. Not too bad, perhaps, except that these are people above fifty: their understanding of financial arithmetic has already largely determined their chances of a decent retirement lifestyle. Three-quarters of the respondents get the inflation question right. Only half get the question on diversification right. Just one-third get all three questions right. Given that responsibility for pension provision is passing inexorably to the individual, these figures ought to be cause for concern.

The problem of pensions is almost perfectly designed to exploit all of the failings of *Homo sapiens*. Cue behavioral finance. The single greatest application of behavioral theory for financial purposes is the use of "auto enrollment" in private pension schemes. By requiring employees to opt out of a scheme rather than make the effort to opt in, auto enrollment takes advantage of people's tendency to dither rather than decide. People who never get around to saving now never get around to opting out. American companies that use auto enrollment report sharp jumps in average participation rates in 401(k) schemes: as much as 60 percentage points higher for employees who have been at a firm for a year. Auto enrollment was introduced in Britain in 2012, and more than 1 million workers have since been enrolled in occupational schemes under the system.[16]

There is a sting, however. Inertia means that people who are automatically opted into a pension scheme also tend to stick with default savings rates. A majority of American companies set this default rate at 3 percent of salary or less, which is less than many employees would choose to save if they were enrolled voluntarily. So the behavioralists have had to fight back with another clever technique known as "auto escalation," an opt-in feature that automatically increases employees' savings rates whenever they get a pay rise until they hit a maximum level of contributions.[17]

By synchronizing contribution increases and salary hikes, this "Save More Tomorrow" option also gets around another human foible known as "loss aversion," which means that people weigh losses more heavily than gains. Loss aversion appears to have very deep neurological roots. In a 2005 study, a trio of academics from Yale introduced a colony of capuchin monkeys to the concept of money. The monkeys were first trained to understand that they could exchange a token for food. Having grasped its purpose, some familiar patterns of behavior emerged. The monkeys responded to price signals, buying more of one food than another when its relative price dropped. One monkey strayed into crime by trying to make off with a full tray of tokens. Another was seen using a token to pay for sex.[18]

More pertinent for our purposes, the monkeys also responded very differently when the food on offer was displayed in different ways. They showed a marked preference, for example, for a researcher who showed them one piece of food and handed that piece over in exchange for a token, compared with a researcher who showed them two pieces of food before trading and always removed one of those pieces when the exchange of the token happened. This experiment and others convinced the researchers that like humans, monkeys weigh losses more than gains.

Monkeys have not yet evolved far enough to invent pensions, but if they did, the Save More Tomorrow program would help. Because take-home pay does not go down when contributions go up, there is no perceived loss of earnings and people are much happier to keep saving. The first application of the program, which was developed by two behavioralists named Shlomo Benartzi and Richard

Thaler, prompted employees at a manufacturer to increase their contribution rates from 3.5 percent to 13.6 percent of salary in only three and a half years. The option is now offered by more than half of the large companies in the United States.[19]

With these encouraging examples to build from, a mini industry devoted to behavioral prompts and nudges is springing up. Academics and institutions are busily conducting experiments that tease out the effects of subliminal cues on savings. In one such example, e-mails were sent to the employees of a large American technology firm. A control group of recipients received an e-mail reminding them of the matching-contribution rules in their 401(k) retirement plans (whereby employers match employee contributions) and telling them how much money they had put into the plan so far that year. The guinea pigs in the trial got e-mails that included extra sentences designed to act as savings cues.[20]

The idea was to test another big behavioral quirk: the effect that exposure to arbitrary numbers, or "anchors," can have on people. The effect was first formally identified by Amos Tversky and Daniel Kahneman, a pair of psychologists whose studies of human decision making laid the foundations for the field of behavioral economics. In a 1974 experiment, they rigged a roulette wheel to stop at either 10 or 65 and then asked people to estimate the percentage of African countries in the United Nations. The subjects were instructed to indicate first whether the roulette-wheel number was higher or lower than their estimate for the proportion of African countries in the UN and then to give their estimate. The roulette number acted as an anchor that dramatically affected their guesses. For half of the participants, the roulette wheel stopped on 10. They gave a median estimate of 25 percent of countries. For the other half, the wheel stopped on 65. Their median estimate was 45 percent.[21]

The researchers in the 401(k) experiment wanted to test whether this anchoring effect could be used to affect savings rates in employees' retirement plans. Some recipients got an e-mail with the following extra sentences in it: "For example, you could increase your contribution rate by A% of your income and get more of the match money for which you're eligible. (A% is just an example, and shouldn't be interpreted as advice on what the right contribution increase is for you.)"

Employees were randomly assigned different values for "A%," ranging from just 1 percent to as high as 20 percent. In other e-mails, employees were given different cues, like the example of savings goals for the year of seven and eleven thousand dollars. The presence of such figures did indeed have an effect on subsequent behavior. Low savings cues actually decreased contribution rates by up to 1.4 percent of income; high cues increased contribution rates by up to 2.9 percent of income. There is scope here for both policy makers and financial providers to use guide ropes of this sort systematically to influence savings behavior.

IDEAS LIKE THOSE of Robert Merton and the behavioralists, allied to changes in statutory and effective retirement ages, can help younger workers with time to build up a savings pot before retirement, or to let compound interest do its stuff. But what about those people already closing in on retirement? Rather than accumulation, what older workers have to get right is "decumulation," the process of running down savings to pay for retirement. This is no easy matter. Spend too much, and you might run out of cash well before you die. Spend too little, and your golden years will be tarnished. People who are paid to think about the industry's future wonder about the potential for an "old people's bank" for the baby boomers, whose services would be explicitly based around budgeting, managed drawdowns of savings, and the like.

In the meantime, the annuity is the obvious answer to the problem of not knowing when you are going to die, but it has its flaws. If you have a small pension pot, an annuity may deliver only a meager stream of income; fixed annuities offer no protection against the effect of inflation; and loss aversion means that people hate the idea of "losing out" to the annuity provider if they die early.

Another option is to squeeze more juice out of the assets that older people do own. The biggest of those is likely to be their houses. In 2009 half of home owners aged sixty-two and older in the United States had at least 55 percent of their net worth tied up in home equity. The most obvious way for a retiree to monetize this investment is by selling the house and either renting or "downsizing" into a smaller house. Downsizing has the effect of releasing larger properties onto the market for the generation behind and of releasing equity for people to invest in liquid financial assets. The AARP Public Policy Institute reports that 80 percent of Americans over the age of fifty are home owners, and more than 80 percent of those aged fifty to sixty-four have home equity. Despite the housing crash, the median amount of home equity for households in the fifty-five to sixty-four age range in 2010 was $100,000; it was $135,000 for those sixty-five and over. A smaller property can also be much cheaper to run once you've moved in: one analysis suggests that a retired person or couple in Britain who sell their three-bedroom home and buy a two-bedroom one would typically save £1,530 ($2,375) through lower utility bills, local taxes, and the costs of maintenance and repairs.[22]

In practice, however, downsizing involves transaction costs that are the equivalent of throwing retirement income away. The really big gains in terms of living standards are available to those who are willing to move to a cheaper area of the country, but a study of older Americans' housing moves found that nearly 60 percent are short-distance moves of fewer than twenty miles. And none of this is to address the simple emotional question of whether people want to leave their family house.[23]

For some people, finance provides another answer: the reverse mortgage. Like many parts of the industry, this is a product with a short history and a checkered reputation but an important future. The idea of the reverse mortgage is for home owners to turn the equity in their house into cash. So let's say you have $200,000 in equity in your house. By taking out a reverse mortgage, you can get a loan for close to that amount from the lender, can stay in the house, and don't have to pay back the loan or the interest until the house is sold or when you die. The proceeds from the transaction are used to pay back the principal and accrued interest. This is a product for people who do have enough money to sustain their lifestyle *if* you count both their liquid and their illiquid assets.

Reverse mortgages sound like a great product for the rich world's retirement crisis. If house prices rise, home owners can sell or refinance and get hold of the additional equity that way. If house prices drop, meaning a sale does not raise enough money to repay the loan, then it is not the home owner's problem. For investors, the risk is that people live for much longer than expected, so money does not come back to them when they plan, and that house prices have fallen in the meantime, so they get less than they loaned. In the United States, which has yet to meet a housing-finance instrument it does not want to subsidize, this is really a risk for the government, which insures lenders against losses for houses up to a maximum loan amount of $625,000. (There are moves afoot to create a private market for home owners who want to tap greater amounts of home equity than that.) The Consumer Financial Protection Bureau, in its 2012 report on reverse mortgages to Congress, concluded that they "have the potential to become a much more prominent part of the financial landscape in the coming decades."[24]

Yet the reverse mortgage has some big obstacles to overcome. The numbers issued since the 2007–2008 crisis have dropped dramatically: some fifty-five thousand Americans took one out in 2012, less than half the number made in 2009. That partly reflects the regulatory environment for banks, as capital constraints lead them to withdraw from the market. But it also reflects the reputational risks associated with the product, which has suffered from some serious PR disasters: in at least one case, title to the house belonged to only one of the resident couple, and when the titleholder died, the surviving spouse was kicked out. "Bank Kicks Little Old Lady Out of House" is the kind of headline any boss would run scared of.

There is a less obvious problem, too: the kids. People around the industry say that there is often a problem with children who do not want to see the family home, their rightful inheritance, pass to a financial institution. Back at MIT, Robert Merton, mind whirring, thinks that the product can be tweaked to meet that need: "What if you had a reverse mortgage where part of the value went to the kids immediately, when they probably need it most? You could even give kids a call option [a right to buy] on the home in case there has been massive house-price appreciation."

THE HOUSE ISN'T the only asset that older people can turn into cash. They can also monetize themselves. The life-settlements industry enables holders of life-insurance policies to sell their policies to an investor for more than what is known as the "cash-surrender value," which is the amount you get back from an insurer if you voluntarily terminate a policy. The investor takes over the policy, keeps paying the premiums, and collects the payout when the original policyholder dies.

The immediate forerunner of today's life-settlements industry was an industry called "viatical settlements," which emerged in the 1980s in response to the AIDS epidemic. The word comes from the Latin *viaticum* for the communion taken before death, and the idea was to enable people whose life expectancy was very limited to sell their insurance policies in order to raise cash for medical expenses and end-of-life care. In an illustration of why this area of investing makes people so uncomfortable, this particular asset lost its appeal when improvements in the treatment of AIDS patients brought about dramatic improvements in their life expectancy.

As the needs of the baby boomers increase and the strains on the public finances worsen, the life-settlements industry is attracting the interest of policy makers. In June 2013 Rick Perry, the

Republican governor of Texas, signed a bill allowing life-insurance policyholders to sell their policies to pay for long-term care without sacrificing their rights to access Medicaid. The bill gives consumers a way of getting hold of more money, while long-term care providers get more seniors paying private-payer rates for longer, and the state saves money for as long as they use private providers. Other states are considering the same regulation.

But the life-settlements industry is also the sort of thing that appears to confirm the worst fears about finance. Not content with gambling with our livelihoods, investors are betting on our lives. That raises some very old worries. The idea of "insured interest" is broadly that an insurance policy is valid if the policyholder gains from the continued existence of the thing being insured. Without that requirement, people could take out insurance on the lives and property of other people and benefit from their death or destruction. (This is exactly the same worry that stalks so-called naked credit-default swaps, in which people can buy protection on a corporate default without actually being exposed to the debt of the company in question.)

Such speculation was common in eighteenth-century Britain, where insurance policies were routinely taken out on public figures. One such was Admiral John Byng, the only British admiral to be executed, after failing to engage the French fleet with sufficient ardor at Minorca in 1756. Admiral Byng's death, at the hands of a firing squad on the deck of his flagship in 1757, was the subject of a bitter dispute: his descendants still petition for a posthumous pardon. Others took a coldly commercial view of the affair: the premiums that people were prepared to pay to take out insurance on the admiral's life varied as his court-martial proceeded and perceptions of his chances of survival ebbed and flowed.

In his book *Betting on Lives,* Geoffrey Wilson Clark points to an even more distasteful event in 1765, when some eight hundred destitute German refugees who had made their way to Goodman's Fields in the East of London began to die from hunger. Today, there would be a charitable appeal. Back then, speculators made bets on the number of Germans alive at a specified future date.[25]

Sometimes, of course, betting on other people's longevity does not pay off. The person with the longest confirmed life span in history was a Frenchwoman named Jeanne Calment, who was born in 1875 and died in 1997 aged 122 years and 164 days. In 1965, at the ripe old age of 90, Calment agreed to sell her apartment to her lawyer, André-François Raffray. Raffray, a then-sprightly 47-year-old, did not pay Calment a lump sum but paid a monthly sum of twenty-five hundred francs until she died. That doubtless sounded like a good bet to Raffray, but when pen met paper he was signing one of the worst contracts in history. Raffray was still paying out when he died from cancer thirty years later, with Calment still firing away at the age of 120.

Whenever financial products are being sold to senior citizens, it is reasonable to worry about the risk of misselling and fraud. Indeed, some entrepreneurs are already trying to develop products that explicitly deal with the problem of deteriorating cognition among older people: True Link Financial, for example, is a Californian start-up aimed at helping senior citizens avoid fraud by developing a debit card that declines withdrawals when predefined limits are triggered.

But life settlements are also a good example of how finance often elicits a one-eyed response. The traded policies have been nicknamed "death bonds" in some quarters. At a congressional hearing in 2009, Paul Kanjorski, a Pennsylvania Democrat, had this to say: "The idea of institutional investors profiting from a person's death seems, to say the least, unsettling and immoral." Such unease is natural, but it is very selective. If Kanjorski finds life settlements unsettling, he ought to dislike the annuity, which converts a pension pot into an income for life. The annuity is another product that pits the individual against the insurer in a wager over the arrival of the grim reaper: if people die earlier than expected, then the effect is to deliver a financial benefit to the insurer. But no one calls annuities "death contracts."

This tendency to regard the unfamiliar as dangerous and the familiar as fine is not restricted to life insurance. The odium heaped on high-frequency trading and the nostalgia for the old days of equity-market trading provide one example. But the scale of the problem of longevity is such that doing nothing is by far the riskier course of action than trying out new ideas. The likes of Merton and Andrew Lo are well aware of the risks of financial experimentation. "Innovation does increase risks of crisis: any successful innovation will run ahead of the infrastructure to support it," says Merton. The question that counts is whether the trade-off is worth it. As the funding model for medical research buckles, and as more and more people head toward retirement with insufficient savings to see them through it in comfort, the answer clearly favors creativity over caution.

CHAPTER 6

EQUITY AND
THE LICENSE TO DREAM

Visit the offices of a start-up, and there'll usually be something self-consciously wacky to see. Someone might be playing table tennis in a desultory, "Look-at-us-being-noncorporate" way. There'll be a hammock. The plants will tweet when they need water. The real mavericks of the start-up world would get everyone to wear suits and work in cubicles.

If the start-up environment sounds formulaic, the job that entrepreneurs do is anything but. The great technological breakthroughs often happen at new firms. And they make an outsized contribution to job growth. New firms are much more likely to fail than older ones: 50–70 percent of business start-ups fail. But those that do survive grow more rapidly than their mature counterparts. The OECD's biennial Science, Technology, and Industry Scoreboard shows that across all the countries it looks at, young small firms (as opposed to established small firms) are disproportionately

147

important to job creation. Young firms with fewer than fifty employees represent only 11 percent of employment but account for more than a third of total job creation in nonfinancial businesses. The figures are yet more striking for even younger businesses. Start-ups account for only 3 percent of total employment in the United States but almost 20 percent of gross job creation.[1]

If you care about employment, in other words, you should care about how to nurture new companies. Finance is fundamental to this challenge. Channeling capital to unproven ventures is by its nature a tougher proposition than funding established businesses. The risks are higher, and the information available to investors is scarcer. These same problems also exist when it comes to funding young people—whether young graduates with entrepreneurial ambitions or students who simply need money to fund themselves through college. The answers that finance has come up with to this problem of funding youth vary for businesses and people. But they have not worked as well as they might.

Let's start with companies. In the ten years before the 2007–2008 crisis, two great, distorting financial events solved the problem of getting money to really young businesses. The first was the dot-com boom, when a wild enthusiasm for online start-ups saw huge amounts of equity flowing to businesses that made no commercial sense at all. Finding money was easier if you were a start-up than if you were a long-standing business with real assets.

The second great distortion was the housing boom of the mid-2000s, which enabled entrepreneurs in many countries to turn their biggest assets—their houses—into cash. Lenders were prepared to use property as security when they extended credit, in the expectation that prices would keep on rising. By marrying data on home ownership and data on house-price shocks, researchers have shown that French entrepreneurs who own their own houses are able to expand their businesses faster if their house values appreciate more quickly. Another study, looking at precrisis America, found that areas with rising house prices experienced significantly bigger increases in both small-business creation and in the number of people working for firms with fewer than ten employees, compared with areas that did not see house-price growth. Housing greased the wheels of the entire economy.[2]

Both of these great distortions are in the past. The equity markets are still prone to bouts of wild excitement over technology firms, but it is nothing like the dot-com days. As for using your home as collateral to fund new businesses, that avenue is less open now that prices have fallen, banks have gotten more cautious, and the problems for lenders of owning the second lien against a property have become clearer.

As we'll discuss in the next chapter, new "peer-to-peer" platforms, which connect lenders and borrowers directly, are springing up to lend to small businesses. But for really new companies—firms that have not yet started generating revenue or are in the very early stages of growth—debt is not the answer. Very young businesses are often not keen on taking on the obligation of debt payments. Servicing debt means a constant drain on the cash flow of the business, and cash is precious. Equity means sacrificing some of the future profits of a business, and potentially control, but it also shovels risk to investors. Investors, too, are likely to prefer equity for really young businesses. Given the failure rate for start-ups and the likelihood of getting no money back at all, the rewards of lending to these businesses are capped by whatever the interest rate is. An ownership stake gives investors the chance to make really big money if a start-up turns into the next Google.

The problem that both sides have to solve, however, is lack of information. Young businesses do not have a lot of data to share or collateral to offer. The financial industry's answer to this conundrum is venture capital, a sector dating back to the founding in 1946 of the American Research and Development Corporation, a publicly traded fund designed to solicit private investment in businesses being run by returning World War II soldiers. Venture capitalists solve the problem of lack of information by conducting exhaustive due diligence on prospective investments. Theirs is a "whites-of-the-eyes" business in which the qualities of the entrepreneur are central to any decision to invest. "Angel" investors, wealthy individuals who put their own money into start-ups, take a similar approach.

In some ways, the venture-capital model has worked well. Between 1999 and 2009, more than 60 percent of "true" IPOs (that is, the ones that are not spinouts, master-limited partnerships, reverse leveraged buyouts, and all manner of other corporate-finance wizardry) were VC backed. Given that only one-sixth of 1 percent of all companies are VC backed, this is a very good record. That said, what is good for the economy may not be good for investors. The successes that VC has notched up—the Facebooks and LinkedIns and Twitters of the world—sit alongside an awful lot of duds. Limited partners in VC funds have done badly overall: since 1997 less cash has been returned to investors than has been put in.[3]

Moreover, the VC model, based as it is on personal relationships, is inherently limiting. Even though there is a lot of institutional money flowing to venture capital, an entrepreneur in Silicon Valley is going to have a better chance of finding funding than an entrepreneur in North Dakota. Things are even worse across the Atlantic: the industry rule of thumb is that young American firms raise twice as much money in each round of financing as European ones—and twice as fast. There are other drawbacks, too. VC firms tend to put in larger chunks of money than very early-stage companies often need. Once on board, the pressure from investors to hit financial targets quickly can mean forcing the pace of expansion beyond what is right. And angel investors, who are a likelier source of small amounts of cash, are not always angelic.

DAVID AND TERESA STEVENS know all about the problem of hunting for cash for a bright business idea. This husband-and-wife duo from the south coast of England founded Guardian Maritime in 2011. Their customers are international shipping firms, and the issue they are trying to solve is maritime piracy. Although the number of attacks on vessels off the coast of Somalia has fallen sharply in recent years, the global threat to shipping remains considerable. The International Maritime Bureau's Piracy Reporting Centre recorded 201 incidents of piracy during the first ten months of 2014. The Stevens' initial product was a complex affair in which captain and crew of a vessel that was under attack could get themselves into a kind of onboard panic room and control the ship remotely from there. But shipowners much preferred to ensure that the pirates didn't embark in the first place.[4]

The next answer that the Stevenses came up with, in 2012, was much less high-tech. The "Guardian" is a plastic device that fits onto the rails of ships and has a large overhang that stops pirates' grappling hooks and ladders from gripping, making it almost impossible for people to climb on board. It is effective, and it is also cheaper than alternatives like decking ships with razor wire every time they leave port. Shipping firms like the product: the Stevenses soon boasted an annual turnover of close to 1 million pounds.

Even so, the firm's fortunes were very precarious. The Stevenses may know a lot about piracy, but their financial decisions had been poor. By their own admission, the couple were of a generation that tried to avoid credit: they had started the business by selling their house and using the proceeds. That had the effect of ruining their credit scores, scaring off banks that were in any case wary of lending in the aftermath of the crisis. An early angel investor, who had gotten 15 percent of the company for a song, was more interested in cracking the whip than helping, according to Mrs. Stevens. With cash needed to pay suppliers, the couple were staring at the prospect of closure by the end of 2013. In desperation, Mr. Stevens searched the Internet for funding options and came across a name he hadn't heard before: Crowdcube.

Crowdcube is an "equity crowdfunding" site on the Internet, a platform that enables start-ups to sell ownership stakes to investors over the Web. In the autumn of 2013, the Stevenses decided to give it a whirl and ended up raising more than £100,000, from sixty new shareholders, in just five days. Helped along by the imminent release of *Captain Philips,* a Tom Hanks film about Somali piracy, they also got a load of publicity. On the back of that, they were approached by a new angel investor offering to buy out their original angel. "We couldn't be happier with how this worked," says Teresa Stevens.

When I visited Crowdcube in late 2013, they had enabled around eighty early-stage companies to raise more than £15 million in equity from ordinary investors over the Web. By September 2014, those numbers had risen to £46 million raised for 165 businesses. Such figures are small in absolute terms, but big enough to attract a lot of attention. Its two founders, Darren Westlake and Luke Lang, regularly take the train up to London from their base in southwestern England to hobnob with politicians; they have even ended up at Buckingham Palace. For a couple of down-to-earth, bordering-on-scruffy guys without a background in the industry, the interest they have generated comes as a surprise. "We didn't set out to transform global finance," says Lang in puzzlement.

Their impact also reaches across the Atlantic. After the stock-market crash of 1929, the 1933 Securities Act put an end to all sorts of financial practices in the United States, including "general solicitation" by private firms—in plain English, advertising investment opportunities to the general public. It may have been fine for ordinary Americans to gamble their money away in lotteries and casinos, but start-ups were a bet too far. Now the constraints are loosening. Since September 2013 private firms in the United States have been allowed to market their offerings widely, so long as the eventual buyers are all "accredited" (that is, rich) investors. The next step is meant to throw open the gates wider still, allowing "nonaccredited" investors to put money into private firms, including start-ups. There will almost certainly be limits to the percentage of a person's income or assets that can be put into start-ups. But that moment is expected to mark the start of a battle royal between a host of new equity-crowdfunding sites to attract investors and entrepreneurs. For the first time since the Depression, ordinary Americans will be able to put their money to work on the front line for fresh ideas and make money if they succeed.

It is not often that Europe can offer the United States a glimpse of the future (the exceptions include aging populations, reality TV formats, and imperial overstretch), but a laxer regulatory environment means that equity crowdfunding has established itself there years before the United States. Platforms have sprung up in Scandinavia, the Netherlands, and elsewhere, but no market is bigger than Britain's. Crowdcube has rivals, but it was the first to launch. Westlake, who had previously set up a couple of technology businesses, got the idea watching a television series called *Dragon's Den,* in which entrepreneurs pitch their ideas to a lineup of angel investors. The series has managed the difficult trick of making business seem interesting to a mass audience. Struck by the thought that he would be prepared to put a few quid into one of the pitches he was watching, Westlake started to ponder the power of a platform that would raise money for entrepreneurs from the crowd.

The result was Crowdcube, which launched in 2011. People who want to raise money for their business put their pitches online, specifying the amount they want to raise in return for a specified chunk of the business. Not everyone gets onto the site: around 70–80 percent of entrepreneurs are told by Crowdcube to provide more information in their business plans. That is often enough to put off the fly-by-night operators and the people who have had a bright idea in the pub.

On the other side of the marketplace are the investors. Crowd-cube is not quite open to all: people either have to self-certify that they are high net-worth individuals or sophisticated investors or have to fill out a questionnaire that is designed to weed out any-one who really doesn't understand the risks of start-up investing. But the bar is not set very high. You get asked things like whether most start-ups (a) succeed or (b) fail, and whether the founders are obliged to pay you back if the company gets into trouble. This is not a test, more like a lengthy reminder that you are very likely to end up losing money if you play the VC game.

None of which will satisfy the skeptics. They argue that a bunch of retail investors putting money into start-ups is, at best, a rec-ipe for locking cash up in an illiquid asset; at worst, a formula for scammers to fleece people; and, in either case, very likely to result in losses. Added to that is the worry that only firms that have not been able to win over the venture capitalists and angels end up looking for money from the crowd. In other words, equity crowd-funding will be the investor of last resort. Felix Salmon, a trenchant columnist, put it like this: "When you open up the dumb money to projects which the smart money has passed on, the outcome is certain, and not pleasant."[5]

THE PHRASE *dumb money* is worth a detour. It is clearly the case that some investors are more sophisticated and knowledgeable than others, but drawing that dividing line is extraordinarily diffi-cult. The crisis showed just how stupid the smart investor can be.

Whereas the dot-com boom could be partly pinned on amateur day traders going mad, the buyers of all those toxic mortgage-backed securities were institutional investors. I recall an IMF official telling me that no line is more arbitrary than that between the sophisticated and unsophisticated investor. Banks have belatedly woken up to that fact: in the wake of the crisis, Goldman Sachs has moved away from treating all its institutional clients as big boys who know what is going on to dividing them into groups that need more or less hand-holding. Municipalities, for instance, may not be allowed to buy or sell derivatives unless these instruments are clearly matched by an underlying interest (a loan that needs hedging, say).

The asset-management industry provides more food for thought. In *The Little Book of Behavioral Investing,* James Montier recounts his experience of running a test among a large group of professional investors. The investors were asked to pick a number between 1 and 100. The winner would be the person who picked the number closest to two-thirds of the average number picked. The results were not particularly flattering to the respondents. Several people plumped for numbers higher than 67. Given the range of possible answers, it is mathematically impossible for a number above 67 to be two-thirds of the average answer. 67 itself is possible, but only if you think that everyone else in the room has chosen 100. Pity the clients who have put their money with these representatives of smart money.[6]

Others in the room tried harder—perhaps a bit too hard. There was a noticeable spike of answers at the value 0. Since two-thirds of 0 is 0, that implies these respondents believed that everyone in the room picked 0. You can see the logic that leads to this guess: if you are always trying to pick a number lower than the average, and everyone in the room knows that this is the point of the game, then you must keep lowering your guess until you can go no further. But it takes a huge leap of faith in people's rationality to assume that everyone will wind up at the same place. (The correct answer in this instance, Montier reports, was 17, two-thirds of the average answer of 26.)

This is a parlor game, of course. What happens when professionals are given the chance to show their skills on home turf, by selecting stocks? In a 2004 study, also cited by Montier, fund managers and psychology students without any financial background were asked to select from a pair of stocks the one that they thought was most likely to outperform the other. The students picked the right stock 49 percent of the time, and the professionals did so just 40 percent of the time. Knowledge is not power.[7]

Again, this may be being unfair. Professional investors make their decisions after analysis, discussion, and reflection, not in artificial psychology experiments. So what does the market tell us? Actively managed funds, in which asset managers make selections designed to beat the market average, have a poor record in comparison with "passive" funds, which aim simply to track benchmark indexes. The active funds attract much higher fees than the passive ones: investors are paying for the potential of outperformance. In an assessment of the performance of active and passive funds at the end of 2012, Standard & Poor's found that over the previous ten years, a majority of active funds had been outperformed by the benchmark index in every single category of American equities. In that same period, the S&P 500 outperformed the HFRX, a measure of hedge-fund returns, every single year, with the exception of 2008, when both fell sharply. In aggregate the fees that hedge-fund investors pay to fund managers were almost certainly higher than the returns they made.[8]

The same applies to venture-capital investors. In an important and self-flagellating report into its own experience of investing in VC funds, the Kauffman Foundation revealed that the majority of the funds it had invested in failed to beat the returns available from the stock markets. Yet it and other investors continued to pour money into the asset class. The Kauffman report blamed providers of capital for continuing to shovel money to funds that they do not properly investigate and for paying them fees that incentivize funds to grow big rather than invest well. There are undoubtedly talented investors out there, and there is certainly a lot of dumbness, but it may not be distributed in the way you expect.[9]

THE AMOUNT OF MONEY flowing through Crowdcube is still small beer in absolute terms. When I visited, no firm that had been funded on the platform had yet managed to realize cash for its investors, via a sale or an initial public offering. One of them, a soap maker called Bubble & Balm, had already gone bust. More start-ups will fold, of course. "We always knew the bad news would come before the good news," says Westlake. It will take time to assess the ability of the crowd to sift good bets from bad.

It is not too early, however, to make some judgments on whether this is just "dumb money." Once registered, investors can browse the site looking at all manner of ideas to change the world and scrutinizing the entrepreneurs behind them. The selection of companies is eclectic, though predominantly geared toward consumers. On the occasions I browsed Crowdcube, I came across firms such as Tabbit, which was touting a smartphone app enabling people to order drinks without having to line up at the bar; GlassFit, a fitness app for Google Glass that aimed to make exercise fun by, for example, showing an avatar up ahead that you can try to overtake; and Castle Three Motoring Company, which manufactured three-wheeled sports cars. Investors can see videos of the founders and their products, read descriptions of the companies, request business plans, and conduct Q&A sessions with the entrepreneurs.

The quality of questioning and feedback was pretty high. For Tabbit, for example, some investors pointed out that other firms had gotten into this area a long time before, prompting a detailed description from the founder about how his product is different. For GlassFit, an app designed for a product that wasn't then available to buy, backers asked what was to stop Google itself from developing the same sort of games. It may not be the same intensive scrutiny that a venture capitalist carries out, but it is not a throw of the dice, either.

What about the fear of herding, the idea that investors will put money into projects that have attracted money simply *because* they have already attracted money? The evidence to date is that the propensity of individual funders to invest does increase rapidly when a project has already won backing. One study into a music-crowdfunding site called Sellaband found that funders were more than twice as likely to invest in artists who reached 80 percent of their funding goal, relative to those who had raised only 20 percent of it. Then again, herding is not necessarily irrational. If popularity is a good in itself, which may well be true for consumer-facing start-ups, then backing the popular ideas makes sense. Indeed, one of the attractions of crowdfunding is that investors can act as ambassadors for the business, promoting and advocating the product more effectively than can a small base of shareholders.[10]

Experienced investors also seem to be using the judgment of the crowd as a form of validation for entrepreneurs' capacity to get things done. Jeff Lynn is an American lawyer who now runs Seedrs, Crowdcube's main rival. A few people have been responsible for a disproportionate amount of the money invested on Seedrs. Lynn says they often tend to come in when they see an idea has gained traction and is already a long way toward reaching its funding goal. "They want to see evidence of people bringing in their own network and generating momentum," he says. "That's a pretty good test of the entrepreneur." It is also a partial answer to a genuine issue with crowdfunding, which is the lack of face-to-face interaction with entrepreneurs. Veterans of the offline venture-capital world stress that they back people as much as ideas. Making an online video gives you only so much of a sense of a person's drive. Persuading a lot of people to part with their cash is a sterner test.

Lynn's concern, an admittedly self-serving one, is less that people will make bad choices when they put money in, more that they will get stiffed when they try to take money out. His big fear is a gigantic success, a Facebook-like venture that has been funded by the crowd when it is small, has taken off, and is approaching a public listing. He worries that later-stage investors in the business would quietly issue equity in order to dilute the stakes held by those early backers. "Everyone would be celebrating but the crowd." Seedrs is designed to deal with this concern, by creating a nominee structure under which Seedrs itself acts as the sole legal representative for investors and thereby ensures that things such as voting rights cannot be changed on the sly. Lynn reckons that the simplicity of having a single shareholder is attractive for entrepreneurs, too, in reducing the number of interlocutors that they have to deal with, and for potential later-stage investors, who want to have as clean a shareholder register as possible.

Seedrs is built in the image of Lynn, the lawyer who cofounded it. He waited to be authorized by the regulator before launching in Britain. In November 2013 Seedrs went live across Europe; it made an acquisition in the United States in October 2014. Its approach is more formal than Crowdcube's, more concerned with what happens after the money is raised; its fees include a slice of the eventual upside from a start-up cashing out. Crowdcube is a business built more in the mold of Westlake and Lang. It operated for a period without being authorized and has been frantically building local partnerships in other countries to try to knit together an international platform for raising start-up equity from the crowd. Its focus is on raising capital, not what happens afterward. "We don't see what we would do after an investment to help the investor or the business," says Westlake. There are as many shareholders as there are investors in a Crowdcube-funded venture, although a handful of bigger backers commonly take "A" shares that entitle them to voting rights. "The risk of a business going bust is the big risk here, not dilution."

This diversity of models is exactly what markets are meant to foster. For investors who want more protection, Seedrs may be more attractive. For those who want to get their pitch out to the most peo-ple, Crowdcube may have the edge. There is room for other models, too: niche platforms aimed at specific types of businesses, for ex-ample, or crowdfunding aimed at social enterprises. It is in the na-ture of new financial markets to evolve quickly, and more change will undoubtedly come. As the number of pitches on crowdfunding sites grows, the harder it will be to come across the best opportuni-ties. Crowdcube has launched a fund that will invest in pitches on the sites, providing investors with a ready-made way of diversifying. Westlake and Lang are also eyeing the possibilities entailed by al-lowing investors on Crowdcube to connect with each other. In time, for example, it might be possible for investors to see what other in-vestors have put money into and to form syndicates with them or to do an Amazon-style recommendations feature, telling investors in a start-up what other businesses their fellow investors have backed.

I would not exaggerate the wisdom of the crowd: it gave us everything from the Nazis to One Direction. It is sensible to cap the amount of money that retail investors can put into start-up in-vesting. But the industry's (admittedly limited) history to date is reassuring. The crowd appears to be no more idiotic than the pro-fessional investors who allocate money blindly to venture capital. It provides another channel for equity to find its way to start-ups, which is a good thing for the rest of us. And it may help to crack open the door to a new way of financing something else with a limited track record and a high risk of failure: young human beings.

WHILE HE WAS STUDYING economics and computer science at Yale University, Paul Gu asked himself the question that eventually confronts every young person: what should he do with his life? The Chinese-born American was keen on the idea of starting his own company, and the most well-trodden route to that future from an East Coast university was first to head to Wall Street and make some money. The obvious choice for a math whiz was a career in quantitative finance: that seemed to offer the right mixture of autonomy, intellectual challenge, and high pay. In the summer of 2011, Gu interned with DE Shaw, an extremely successful algorithmic-trading firm. But something was missing. As much as he might rationally accept that this firm and others like it were adding value to the capital markets, he did not feel an emotional connection to what he was doing.

Gu is the kind of person who does not lack for options. He was one of the first batch of Thiel fellows, twenty people under twenty who were each given one hundred thousand dollars to skip college for two years and pursue their ambitions in a program funded by Peter Thiel, a guru of technology investing whose résumé includes founding PayPal and backing Facebook. So Gu headed to Silicon Valley, where he worked for six months developing a variety of random Web applications. As he turned business ideas over in his head, he was drawn to a very basic financial problem for young people.

As we discussed in the opening chapter, people have two forms of capital: they have financial capital, which is the money they actually accumulate, and they have human capital, which is their potential to make money through their future earnings. These two forms of capital are out of sync. Old people have depleted their human capital, but they should have accumulated financial capital. Young people have a lot of human capital but not much cash. Finance is what bridges the gap between these two. The student loan is a good example. The person borrowing may be someone with no skills, no experience, and no money; the person paying back should have acquired a bit more of each.

But there is a problem with taking on debt now in order to pay it back with future income. Borrowing may help people to navigate across periods of time, but it does not help with future states. The obligation to repay remains the same whether you are earning nothing or a fortune. In economist-speak, the risk inherent in future earnings is borne by the borrower. That is a problem for students and fresh graduates just as it is for new companies.

Some countries have acknowledged this problem in the way they finance student loans, by having an income threshold below which debt repayments are suspended. But that option is not always available, and in the United States in particular, the debt is very sticky: unlike other forms of borrowing, student loans cannot be discharged in bankruptcy. As well as making higher education less appealing for lower-income adolescents, this also makes it harder for debt-laden new graduates to choose the uncertain payoffs associated with entrepreneurialism rather than, say, a hefty monthly paycheck on Wall Street.

There is an alternative, however. Why not take a leaf from the way that young companies are funded and use equity rather than debt to finance students or young graduates? Instead of creditors demanding a fixed payment, equity investors would take a specified proportion of someone's future earnings, whatever they might be. This was the idea that drew the attention of Paul Gu. Because payments rise and fall depending on how much money you earn, he reasoned, this ought to be a far better way to encourage youngsters to take the risk of going down the entrepreneurial path.

The idea is not a new one. Milton Friedman, a celebrated economist, proposed a financial instrument that would allow people to buy a part of a student's future income in a 1955 paper called "The Role of Government in Education." In 1971 Yale University experimented with an income-contingent financing program in which students would repay a very thin slice of annual income, whatever level it was, until the loan was repaid. The program was not a success, in part because individuals were grouped into a cohort in which each member had responsibility for the payments of the others. The effect was to introduce a lot of "correlation risk" into the arrangement: one person's default pushed up the payments of everyone else, making it likelier that someone else would default, pushing up the payments of everyone else, and so on.[11]

Subsequent attempts to introduce equity-like funding for education have been more successful. The pioneer in the use of what are known as "human-capital contracts" is Lumni, which was founded in 2003 and has so far financed thousands of students in Chile, Colombia, Mexico, and the United States by creating a variety of funds for investing in pools of young people. In return, students commit to pay investors a fixed percentage of their income for a ten-year period after they graduate. The fund structure does not repeat the Yale mistake of collective financial responsibility but does allow for diversification of risk: there is more chance that a low-earning graduate will be canceled out by a high-earning one. It also enables the creation of different types of funds. Some are nonprofit; others emphasize financial returns; some are funded by companies looking to invest in high-potential employees, and others are for specific universities. A German firm called CareerConcept, founded in 2002, uses a similar model of educational funding.

Ten years on, Paul Gu reckoned the time was right to give the market another kick. It turned out he was not the only one in Silicon Valley to be thinking about the stifling effects of student debt on risk taking. Dave Girouard, a former Google employee, was thinking along similar lines. When the two were introduced by mutual friends, they joined forces, and a new firm called Upstart was born. The business was designed to provide an online platform on which backers can meet with young people, or "upstarts," pitching for funds. Some upstarts simply used the platform to repay student debt, converting one form of financing for another; others raised funds to help them work toward specific entrepreneurial ideas. In return, backers got a slice of their income for a period of five or ten years.

At almost exactly the same time that Upstart was being started up, in 2012, another company called Pave was being launched on the other side of the country. When I visited their trendy open-plan office in the SoHo district of New York a year later, its founders— two former Goldman Sachs employees named Sal Lahoud and Oren Bass and an ex-Facebooker named Justin Mitchell—made the same argument as Gu: that the need to meet debt repayments is bound to cramp the willingness of young people to take risks. The entrepreneurs and artists of the future would become desk jockeys instead of pursuing their dreams. "Silicon Valley is good at supporting people with ideas, but why should it be the only place in the country that can do that?" says Mitchell. "What about a platform that could help all industries, not just technology, and that could address the stifling effect of student debt on long-term thinking?"

FINANCE IS LITTERED with great ideas that fail to soar. The fact that the market for educational equity hasn't really taken off in the past is cause for skepticism. Sure enough, in May 2014, Upstart announced that it was abandoning its experiment with what are known as "income-share agreements" or "human-capital contracts" in order to concentrate on lending products. Pave has since also put its equity product on hold in order to concentrate on the bigger, more established market of consumer lending to young graduates. The problems they encountered were typical ones for a start-up: the pressure to make a return within a reasonable time frame sat uneasily with a model where people paid back investors from unpredictable incomes over many years. At the same time, there was a lot of capital sloshing into new forms of lending (see the next chapter).

Novelty was also a problem for income-share agreements. New products must surmount a range of regulatory and tax barriers. There are no data with which to reassure the providers of capital. And the youngsters themselves are also flying blind. Everyone has had experience of taking out a loan—or knows someone who has had that experience. But almost no one can give you guidance about whether to give away a share of your future earnings. And there is something conceptually troubling about pledging a proportion of your future income to an investor. Isn't this just a type of indentured servitude, a form of bondage common in the American colonial states in which young migrants would be required to work for an employer for a fixed number of years in order to pay off the costs of their journey from Europe? The idea of someone owning the fruits of your labor doesn't feel very progressive. In fact, it is hard to understand why a form of payment that flexes when your circumstances do, rather than imposes an unbending obligation to repay, is the more constraining of liberty.

Even if Upstart and Pave have moved away from equity and toward debt, there are nonetheless good reasons to believe that the market is edging closer to reality. In just over a year of offering the contracts, Upstart's backers made $3.5 million worth of offers to 320 upstarts and began to crack the code for how to make the market work. Providers such as Lumni continue to operate. Pave's Bass says that he still sees a future for its equity product, if regulatory barriers (which, for example, prevent retail investors from putting money in) can be lowered. Most important of all, the US government has begun to get seriously interested in alternatives to student debt.

Official encouragement matters enormously to new markets. Looking back at the early days of some of the more demonized elements of the financial landscape, it is striking how often governments and multilateral bodies have acted as midwives to new products. They have the financial resources to get things off the ground quickly, and because they are not subject to the same commercial imperatives as the private sector, they are willing to experiment. The role of the US government in promoting the securitization markets is well known. Ginnie Mae, a government-owned corporation, was the first to sell securities backed by a portfolio of mortgage loans in 1970; the first collateralized mortgage obligation was issued by Fannie Mae in 1983. The first currency and interest-rate swap was written in London between the World Bank and IBM, in an agreement that saw the World Bank exchange its surplus dollars for the computing firm's stock of unwanted Swiss francs and deutsche marks. The first credit-default swap transaction, in 1994, saw the European Bank for Reconstruction and Development, a multilateral organization ostensibly dedicated to funding the transition economies of Eastern Europe, insure JP Morgan against the risk of Exxon defaulting.[12]

Political goals are also important in driving financial markets forward. The obvious example is the policy of successive American administrations of promoting home ownership. Now politicians are looking at the way students are being funded through college and finding that it looks less and less sustainable.

At a time when American households are paying down debt, student loans are the only form of consumer borrowing that has gone up since 2008. The total amount of student debt outstanding in the United States is now above $1 trillion. Only mortgage debt is bigger. Both the number of student borrowers and the average loan balance increased by 70 percent between 2004 and 2012. The Congressional Budget Office reckons that the government will loan students another $1.4 trillion over the next decade. This growth has been driven by a number of factors. The cost of a college education per student has risen by almost five times the rate of inflation since 1983. The number of people participating in tertiary education has nonetheless increased, as has the length of time students spend in college and graduate school.[13]

Delinquency rates have been rising, too: figures from the New York Federal Reserve showed that about 17 percent of borrowers were more than ninety days overdue on student-loan repayment in 2012, compared with less than 10 percent in 2004. Being behind on student debt has inevitable consequences for the ability of students to gain access to other forms of credit, most obviously a mortgage. That is logical enough: lenders shouldn't be extending credit to people who are already struggling. But even people who are current on student-loan payments appear to be more credit constrained.

Another piece of analysis by the New York Fed showed that between 2003 and 2009, home-ownership rates were significantly higher for thirty-year-olds with a history of student debt than for those without student debt. That situation has changed radically. Although thirty-year-olds in both groups have seen their home-ownership rates fall sharply since 2008, the decline has been far more precipitous for those carrying student debt: indeed, thirty-year-olds with no history of student debt are now more likely to have a mortgage than those with such a history. The same crossover has occurred among twenty-five-year-olds who have financed a car purchase. Part of the reason for that is a stricter underwriting environment, in which higher debt-to-income ratios are taken much more seriously by lenders.[14]

You might look at these changes and shrug. Home ownership was given too much emphasis in the boom; it ought not to be a benchmark. The state of the economy is bound to be having an impact on employment, earnings, and borrowing capacity. It is a good thing that lenders are being more stringent. All of that is true, but there is still something very corrosive about this picture. The whole point of borrowing in order to pay for a college education is that it delivers an overall economic return for students. One recent paper estimated that a typical college graduate will enjoy a level of annual consumption that is 38 percent higher than that of an otherwise identical high school graduate. But the payoff is less secure than it once was and is taking longer to arrive. Part of the reward ought to be easier access to credit. It should make more sense for a mortgage lender to loan money to a graduate because of the higher lifetime-earning power that a college education delivers, for example. But at the moment, the industry is more focused on current debt than future income.[15]

Some argue that it makes sense for fewer people to choose to go to college. But finance helps to determine how free that choice really is. The process of bank-branch deregulation that swept the United States between the 1970s and 1990s led to greater competition between lenders and to lower interest rates for borrowers. That in turn enabled lower- and middle-income families to borrow more from banks to finance college educations for their kids. One study found that easier access to credit following branch deregulation accounted for 20 percent of the total increase in college enrollments between 1972 and 1992.[16]

Now credit constraints are biting again. Family income has become a much more important determinant of college attendance over time in the United States. As the costs of tuition and the burden of student debt rise, the harder it becomes in relative terms for the offspring of low-income families to make the decision to go to college. That is partly because poor students will need to borrow more to fund themselves. Evidence from the United Kingdom shows that on graduation, the poorest students are substantially more indebted than the richest.[17]

Policy makers are slowly waking up to the problem. The state of Oregon grabbed attention in the summer of 2013 when its legislature approved a commission to study the idea of not charging students at state universities tuition fees in return for repaying the state a proportion of their earnings. Federal lawmakers have mooted the possibility of funding pilot projects to test the idea in other states, too. An even bigger moment came in April 2014, when two US senators, Marco Rubio and Tom Petri, introduced legislation that would provide a legal framework for income-share agreements, specifying the maximum length of such contracts and capping the amount of income that a young person can commit to give an investor. "These plans would help all students get the financing they need—including students from disadvantaged backgrounds—but without the anxiety that comes with traditional loans," said Petri in a statement at the time.

AT THE SAME TIME that policy makers are becoming more intrigued by the idea of income-share agreements, the technological landscape is shifting. The example of firms like Kickstarter, Crowdcube, Lending Club (discussed in the next chapter), and others is habituating people to the idea of funding strangers over an online platform. And the availability of data online means that firms like Upstart can analyze the likely earnings power of youngsters in more sophisticated ways than ever before. The first thing Paul Gu did when he had the idea for equity-funded education was crunch some numbers. Public data from a couple of longitudinal studies showing the long-term relationship between education and income in the United States enabled him to build what he describes as "a simple multivariate regression model"—you know the sort, we've all built one—and work out the relationships between things such as test scores, degrees, and first jobs on later income.

That model has since grown into something whizzier. An applicant's education, SAT scores, work experience, and other details are pumped into a proprietary statistical model, which looks at people with comparable backgrounds and generates a prediction of that person's personal income. Upstart now uses these data to underwrite loans to younger people—who often find it hard to raise money because of their limited credit histories. But the model was initially used to determine how much money an applicant could raise for each percentage point of future income they gave away. Say the model determined a funding rate of fifteen thousand dollars for every 1 percent of income. The applicant then used this number to decide how much money to raise, up to a maximum of 7 percent of earnings. So in our example, the "upstart" might have chosen to raise seventy-five thousand dollars in return for 5 percent of income. Pave also offered its youngsters, whom they call "prospects," guidance on what percentage of income to give away based on historical analysis of salaries.

Like every new financial instrument, however, human-capital contracts have to work very hard to balance the interests of buyer and seller. In theory an equity-based investment in education puts the interests of backer and youngster in perfect alignment—a higher income benefits both parties—whereas a creditor is apathetic about a borrower's income beyond a certain threshold. But in practice, this is a market bedeviled by uncertainty. Far from being enslaved by a human-capital contract, a young person has the option to change careers entirely. You might think you are backing a high-earning computer programmer, but it turns out that your money is funding a low-earning chemistry teacher. The information asymmetry that all markets must grapple with is particularly great when it comes to investing in people: no investor can hope to understand the aspirations, integrity, and self-discipline of a young person like the young person himself. With a traditional loan, the asymmetry still exists, but the obligation to repay at least offers greater protection to the interests of the investor.

Information asymmetry goes hand in hand with a problem known as "adverse selection." Imagine that the year is 2003, and an investor decides to put her money into a promising young Harvard undergraduate named Mark Zuckerberg. As the years roll on, it becomes clear that the investor has made a spectacularly good decision: Zuckerberg's social-networking site, Facebook, is steaming toward a public listing, and a small share of his annual income is still a big amount of money. But what if Zuckerberg decides to pay himself a nominal salary during these early years in order to avoid handing over dollops of cash unnecessarily? More pertinent, wouldn't someone like Zuckerberg have had enough confidence in his own abilities to have avoided an equity contract in the first place? If you think you are going to earn a lot of money, it makes more sense to take on a fixed nominal debt. That reasoning makes it likely that the people most likely to earn a lot of money will stay away, and the people most likely to make a disappointing income will flood in. This is another version of the criticism made of equity crowdfunding: that the best opportunities will be picked off by the experts, and only the dud companies will be left for the crowd.

One way around this problem is to increase the level of contact between the providers and recipients of capital so they can assess each other properly before any investment decision is made. Another is to diversify investors' portfolios so that a bad outcome for one graduate has more chance of being balanced by a better outcome for another. These two approaches are in some senses at odds: having more investees means greater diversification but also reduces the chance of close interaction. The Lumni model is a fund structure: it offers the benefits of diversification at the cost of knowing the individual students as well, which means the youngsters forgo the benefits of a mentoring relationship. The models adopted in their old incarnations by Pave and Upstart allowed for closer interaction, but investors ended up concentrating their risks on fewer individuals as a result.

The critical question is how many, or how few, is enough to feel reasonably confident that your investees will in aggregate earn what is expected of them and deliver their backers a decent return. Gu reckons the number is surprisingly small: his calculations suggested that a pool of ten to twenty upstarts could give investors high confidence that they had a sample that would match the predictions made by Upstart's model. His logic is that wages are a much less volatile asset than they first appear. About 40 percent of start-up companies fail within three years, and that number rises to 65 percent by year ten. The chances of an individual failing to earn their expected income is lower.[18]

What about the issue of adverse selection? A cap on the total absolute amount of income that can be given away is one answer to the Zuckerberg problem—Upstart used to set a limit of five times the amount raised, for example. But Gu's model was also designed to do away with this problem by enabling people with higher income potential (based on where and what they studied, for example, or how well they did in college) to raise more money for every percentage point of income shared than those with lower income potential. These differences in funding rates incentivize people to participate no matter what their forecast earnings. Gu has been critical of the initial thinking in Oregon's mooted "Pay It Forward" plan precisely because it does not distinguish between differences in likely earnings potential. Because they would be paying out a fixed percentage of income, higher earners would end up paying much more for their educations than low earners. Upstart reckons that the top quartile of earners from Oregon State University would pay at least two and a half times what the lowest quartile would pay.

Skeptics will point to another worry. Human-capital contracts would inevitably encourage investors to chase the highest potential earners, exacerbating the problem of bright, young people being funded to head to unproductive careers on Wall Street. This book argues that a career in finance is more socially useful than it is currently given credit for, but in any case Gu's intuition was precisely the reverse: that a form of financing that does not impose a fixed repayment would lead to more risk taking in career choices, not less. Even if he is wrong on that, a risk-based pricing model is an important way to inject some cost discipline into higher education. As for what would happen to the degrees that may lead to lower-income careers that we all value as a society—teaching, health care, social work, and so on—the government could still choose to subsidize these fields, but the subsidy would at least be more transparent.

Any new financial instrument must also negotiate multiple legal and regulatory hurdles. Sharing your income with another person is a new idea, which means thinking through contractual issues from scratch. Enforceability is one obvious issue: how does an investor know how much money a prospect is making, and how can claims be enforced if payment is not forthcoming? One answer is to use tax returns to verify income and enforce contracts; an increasing trend toward the automatic exchange of tax information across borders helps alleviate the risk of students moving to another country to hide income. But this issue does help to explain the value of collateral in resolving many of the hurdles that financial instruments face, especially ones that stretch over many years. It is much easier for mortgage providers to bet on someone's future earnings when there is an immovable bit of security (a house) on hand to provide backup in the event of default. Collateral can also help the borrower, and not just by reducing the cost of borrowing. Provided he is not in negative equity, a mortgage holder has the option of getting rid of his debts by selling his property and paying back the bank. Collateral offers the borrower an exit route. Human capital, the economic value embodied in each of us, is the ultimate illiquid asset.

It will clearly take a lot of time for the concept of human-capital contracts to become a routine part of the financing landscape. It is easier to make this model work for people who have already graduated and want to raise money for the next stage of their careers than to extend it to the financing of undergraduate degrees, where the amount of data that can be drawn on to predict future income is necessarily lower. But the growth of equity crowdfunding for companies offers some hope to similar ventures in education. And after a period in which finance devoted an enormous amount of energy to increasing the amount of debt that we take on, a little bit of fresh thinking about equity is always welcome.

CHAPTER 7

PEER-TO-PEER LENDING AND
THE FLAWS OF FINANCE

Renaud Laplanche is a soft-spoken Frenchman living in San Francisco who, by the mid-2000s, had already set up and sold an enterprise-software business to Oracle. Laplanche was a prompt payer of his outstanding credit-card balance but noticed on his credit-card bill that if he carried over any of his balance to the next month, it would be subject to an interest rate of almost 19 percent. That seemed very high, particularly since he was getting such a paltry return on his deposit account at the bank. Someone was making a lot of money out of this gap.

The rest of us might mutter a bit and then move on to something important like watching reruns of *The West Wing*. Laplanche's response was to set up another business. "A very wide spread is always a signal to an entrepreneur that there is an opportunity," he says. His new firm, launched in 2007, was called Lending Club. It has since won an investment from Google and attracted the likes of Larry Summers, a former Treasury secretary, and John Mack, a former boss of Morgan Stanley, to its board. The company was valued at close to $5 billion in 2014, and an initial public offering, in the works as this book was being completed, was due to make Lending Club known to a lot more people.

Lending Club is the leading light in the "peer-to-peer lending" industry. That name is becoming a bit of a misnomer, for reasons that will become clear, but the concept is simple. Banks intermediate the flow of credit: their job is to sit in between borrowers and lenders. Your deposits accumulate in banks; the banks then take this money and their other liabilities and decide how to loan it out. Your money is going to fund other borrowers; it's just that you don't realize it.

Lending Club and other peer-to-peer lenders use technology to match borrowers and investors directly. Borrowers can pitch for funds to savers on the Lending Club website; those savers can choose whom to loan money to. Without the costs of legacy information technology (IT) systems and branch networks that weigh down the banks, Lending Club can ensure a lower interest rate for borrowers than they would normally get: the average rate that borrowers were paying on loans in 2013 was 14 percent, well inside credit-card charges. Allowing for a default rate of 4 percent, and Lending Club's servicing fees, the returns to investors were 9–10 percent, not too shabby given how low interest rates have been.

Growth has been explosive. By December 2012, Lending Club had surpassed $1 billion in loans taken out since its launch in 2007. It had doubled that by the start of July 2013, hit the $3 billion mark by December of that year, and surpassed $6 billion by the end of September 2014. That sort of heft puts it well ahead of rivals. It also reflects what economists like to call "network effects." A bigger marketplace attracts more borrowers and investors. It also increases liquidity for investors looking to sell off their loans before they mature.

Lending Club is one among a whole series of peer-to-peer start-ups. Its biggest rival in the consumer arena is another San Francisco–based firm called Prosper, which stuttered for a few years but is also growing extremely fast. Across the Atlantic, Zopa, a London-based firm, can lay claim to being the industry pioneer: it has been going since 2005 and focuses on "prime" (that is, the most creditworthy) borrowers. Its British competitors include RateSetter, a platform set up in 2009 by a former employee of Lazard, an investment bank.

Consumer credit is only one application of the peer-to-peer lending model, however. At Relendex, British savers can club together to loan money for commercial mortgages on things such as offices or warehouses—the rental income from the property provides their interest payments. Funding Circle is a British platform that is aimed at connecting lenders with small businesses, which have suffered a shortage of credit as the big banks have retrenched. The site is growing fast: in July 2013 savers had loaned British small businesses a total of £124 million; by November 2013 that number had gone up to £173 million; by November 2014 it was at £435 million. Its product offering is expanding to enable small businesses to borrow against the security of assets. Its geographical horizons are also widening. Funding Circle is now pushing into the US market, where it will come up against Lending Club, which is also moving into small-business loans.

Student debt is another promising field. As we saw in the previous chapter, Upstart and Pave have moved from equity financing into the field of lending to youngsters with limited credit histories. New York–based CommonBond is one of several platforms lending to current students and consolidating the debts of recent graduates. David Klein, one of the platform's cofounders, had initially thought of doing an equity product for this market, but dropped the idea for some familiar reasons. "Our market research showed that people associated it with indentured servitude. It got a visceral reaction, and we don't need that kind of baggage in our product," he says. "We also worried about adverse selection: people who are really confident in their earning ability might stay out of the platform because it is more expensive to give up equity than debt." By lending to MBA students and graduates, it could cream off a creditworthy population of borrowers with proven earning power, match them with alumni and other investors, and offer them a lower interest rate even than the government. It too has been growing by leaps and bounds. An initial $40 million fund was used to finance forty students at the Wharton Business School; by mid-2014 the platform had raised a second $100 million fund and was lending to graduates in a range of programs and schools around the United States.

Debt is not the only application of the peer-to-peer principle. Equity crowdfunding works along the same lines. There are now tentative stabs at peer-to-peer insurance, most notably by a German firm called Friendsurance, which started up in Berlin in 2010.

Under the Friendsurance model, large claims are still the domain of conventional insurers, but the cost of smaller claims—the "deductible" or "excess" amount that a policyholder has to pay out before an insurer does—is shared within a small circle who, in effect, insure each other. A chunk of the premiums they pay is put into a pool to cover these smaller claims; whatever is not claimed is returned at the end of the year. Social insurance of this sort ought to reduce fraud—friends tend not to cheat on each other—and thus costs for the larger insurers who take care of the bigger claims.

ALL OF THIS ACTIVITY looks interesting, but does it really matter? The numbers involved are still tiny, after all. Lending Club is the leading light in the industry, yet its $6 billion of loan originations by 2014 compares with outstanding credit-card debt of $850 billion in the United States and total outstanding consumer debt of more than $11 trillion. Skeptics wonder if the rise of peer-to-peer platforms is a postcrisis phenomenon, an emotional backlash against the banks that will fade as anger against Wall Street does. But the evidence suggests that the upstarts of finance are built to last.

One big clue is the type of money they are attracting. Hang around the industry long enough, and you're bound to hear someone talk grandly about the "democratization of finance." But the platforms also offer a way for big investors to get direct access to unsecured consumer-credit products. Institutional investors now account for more than two-thirds of loan volumes on Lending Club; insurers and sovereign-wealth funds have assigned pots as big as $100 million. Securitizations have already occurred: a hedge fund called Eaglewood Capital that was set up to invest in Lending

Club loans bundled some of them into a securitized offering in the autumn of 2013. SoFi, another peer-to-peer lender specializing in student loans, won an investment-grade rating for a securitization from Standard & Poor's in July 2014. Providers of capital to CommonBond include some famous names from the old wing of the industry, among them Vikram Pandit, a former chief executive of Citigroup.

Ordinary savers do still provide an important source of funding. Borrowers like the idea of being loaned to by individuals rather than faceless money managers, and retail money is a stable source of funding for the platforms, which have to ensure that the demand for loans and the supply of capital is kept in balance. Laplanche recalls the effect of the Standard & Poor's downgrade of the US sovereign credit rating in August 2011, when retail money began coming onto the platform as people panicked about the stock market. "We were the flight-to-safety option for many retail investors," he says. "The flip side was that we saw redemption requests from a couple of hedge funds."

But the flow of institutional money means that the term *peer-to-peer* has long ceased to do justice to the scale and professionalization of the business. Lending Club itself doesn't use the term, says Laplanche, "just like Facebook doesn't call itself a 'social network.'" Some have taken to using labels like "direct lending" and "marketplace lending" instead. "We are a more efficient way of consumer lending and capital allocation" is the description Laplanche offers. That provides another clue to why these platforms have a bright future: they are designed to address some of the flaws of mainstream finance.

The years following the 2007–2008 crisis have produced pages and pages of new regulations on capital, liquidity, derivatives, pay, and resolution regimes, to name just a handful of areas. The aim of these rules is twofold: first, to make sure that banks do not get into such terrible trouble again and, second, to ensure that when there is another crisis, the bill is not passed to the taxpayer. A lot of different weapons are being deployed in the service of these objectives, and despite the cries of those who say nothing has been done to hurt the banks, they are having a powerful effect.

The two most important levers that regulators have to pull are liquidity and equity. Bank runs are not the only way that creditors can bring banks to their knees. Banks borrow short term in a lot of different markets and from a lot of different sources of capital. They borrow in repurchase, or "repo," markets, pledging securities as collateral in return for cash; they borrow from money-market funds; they use commercial paper, a short-term capital-market instrument, to raise money; and so forth. When a debt comes due, the banks' working assumption is that they can roll it over, either borrowing again from the original creditor or using funds from someone else to pay him off. When liquidity freezes, as it did in the summer of 2007, that game is up. Banks have to sell assets quickly in order to realize the cash to meet their maturing debts, and the process of dumping assets drives their prices down, causing losses that make creditors even more unwilling to lend.

Liquidity risk is the sort of thing bankers learn about on day one of the job. But the long boom before the bust inured many institutions to this risk. Since the crisis, regulators (and executives) have gotten wiser. The funding profiles of the banks are changing as a result. Banks that previously depended on short-term whole-sale funding, and found they could no longer roll over their debts when credit first crunched in 2007, are now emphasizing deposits and longer-term funding from the capital markets. Remember that deposits are considered "sticky" because they are insured; long-term funding is safer because issuers do not have to face the markets immediately in the event of a shock.

The other big lever that regulators have pulled is the one marked "equity." Equity is also known as risk capital, because it is the layer of capital that is designed to absorb losses. For a home owner, it is the money you put down as a deposit; for a company, it is the money invested by shareholders. Equity is the buffer that protects banks from disaster when things go wrong. When profits are high, equity wins. When losses mount, equity loses. It is the bit of the capital structure where risk and reward are highest.

Over the long run, banks have progressively been running down the amount of equity that they use. Prior to the founding of the Federal Reserve in 1913 and the Federal Deposit Insurance Corporation (FDIC) in 1933, the amount of equity American banks had on their balance sheets ranged from 13–16 percent of total assets. By 2007 the industry was running with an equity-to-assets ratio of 3.8 percent. The Americans were models of prudence compared with European banks: the Royal Bank of Scotland, for a while the world's largest bank by assets, had an equity "buffer" of just 2 percent in 2007. At that level of leverage, a loss of two dollars on a one-hundred-dollar portfolio wipes out all the bank's capital.[1]

Regulators are now stuffing more capital into the system and ensuring that it is high quality. Previously, banks could count all sorts of different instruments toward their capital requirements. Now regulators emphasize pure equity, so that the capital structure is founded on a thicker layer of funding whose capacity to absorb losses is unquestioned. The amount of equity that banks need is a matter of fierce, often ideological, debate. But wherever the gauge ends up, it will be a lot higher than it was before the crisis.

What does all this have to do with Lending Club and the other new financial platforms? Not much: they are built to sidestep both of these risks. And that is exactly why they have gained the attention of regulators. A platform like Lending Club or Prosper is not running a balance sheet in which it incurs debts in order to be able to fund lending of its own. Rather, it is acting as a marketplace in which borrowers and lenders can meet and transact. If there are defaults on a bank's loan book, its creditors still expect to be paid back. If there are defaults on a Lending Club loan, the investor is the one who suffers. Some peer-to-peer platforms do have mechanisms to alleviate this risk for investors: RateSetter and Zopa run provisioning funds in which they set aside reserves that can be tapped in the event of defaults so that any shortfalls can be filled. But the platforms themselves are not intermediating the risk in the way that banks do.

The new platforms also mitigate the problems associated with maturity transformation, the banks' trick of turning short-term funding into long-term lending. If an investor funds a three-year consumer loan, she can't demand the money back after a month or a year or two years like a depositor can from a bank. The borrower will not face a sudden call for cash and the scramble to raise money that this entails. The mismatch that sits right at the heart of what

banks do is not present. "We don't have to manage maturity transformation," says Laplanche. "We have a perfectly matched market
in terms of assets and liabilities. There is no eight-to-one leverage.
We are derisking the banking system."

That is a seductive message for regulators. Andy Haldane, a
Bank of England official with a deserved reputation for free thinking, has wondered aloud whether the new technology platforms
could end up squeezing out the middleman altogether. His interest
is in shoring up the fragility of a system built on maturity transformation and leverage. But the even bigger reasons to think that these
platforms can keep growing are their affordability and convenience.

Banks have receptionists to outfit, marble floors to polish,
branch networks to run, staffs to pay, capital buffers to maintain,
compliance regimes to observe, and legacy IT systems to cobble
together. Just getting into a bank's headquarters can be an ordeal.
On my first visit to the offices of Morgan Stanley in New York, the
only identification I had on me with a picture was a membership
card for Legoland, a theme park. It featured a grainy photo of me
and an enormous Lego figure carrying a large wrench. I proffered it
to the security guards, and it took three of them, and a long whis-
pered conversation about what the guy with the wrench signified,
before I was allowed in.

Visit the offices of the new platforms, and the cost advantage
they wield becomes obvious. At Zopa, for example, youthful-
looking teams sit in sections: a few people to carry out IT development, another group to screen would-be borrowers for credit risk,
a couple of people to chase up late payers. Over in San Francisco,
Laplanche reckons that the operating expense ratio (a measure that

expresses a company's running costs as a proportion of its revenues) for a credit-card company like Capital One is about 7 percent; for Lending Club it is below 2 percent and dropping.

The importance of speed and convenience cannot be underestimated. Samir Desai is the chief executive of Funding Circle, the platform for small and medium-size enterprises. Although borrowing costs on Funding Circle are lower than those with the banks, price is not the main allure. "Applying for money from the banks takes too long and is too painful," he says. To illustrate the advantage that an online platform has over a bank, he points out that half of Funding Circle's loan applications come outside business hours. A survey of Funding Circle borrowers carried out in 2013 found that 60 percent of them had approached a bank for a loan before finding their way to the platform; asked why these bank applications had not been completed, the top answer was that the process took too long.[2] When I visited Funding Circle in 2013, the average time it took for them to screen a borrower's application was forty-eight hours. Once a borrower was listed, it took just over six days for the loan to be funded. Those times will doubtless have shortened since. At banks the process can take weeks, as decisions bounce from department to department.

Banks are also hamstrung by something known as the innovators' dilemma: the desire to protect existing income streams rather than invent products that may be better. For another example of this problem, look away from debt to foreign exchange and northeast from Zopa's London offices to the fashionable area of Shoreditch. Here in a renovated tea warehouse, you can find another set of people with big ambitions and a low opinion of mainstream finance.

Laplanche was motivated to start Lending Club by his credit-card bill; Taavet Hinrikus was disgruntled for a different reason.

Back in the 2000s, Hinrikus moved from his native Estonia to London. He was still being paid in Estonia in euros but had expenses to meet in pounds in London. Transferring money between his Estonian and British bank accounts stuck him with hefty commissions and unfavorable exchange rates. Hinrikus was not the only one in that situation. A friend of his, Kristo Käärmann, had the same problem in reverse: he worked in London and was paid in pounds, but had a euro-denominated mortgage to pay back in Estonia.

So the two decided to sideline the banks by swapping money directly into each other's accounts: Käärmann paid pounds into Hinrikus's sterling account, and Hinrikus paid euros into Käärmann's euro account. They worked out the appropriate exchange rate by using the midmarket rate published on Reuters and saved themselves hundreds of pounds in foreign-exchange fees.

Hinrikus, a T-shirt-wearing, mild-mannered Estonian with a beard, may not seem like an obvious threat to mainstream banks. But he also happened to be the first employee of Skype, the service that lets you make calls over the Internet for free. Skype at the time was based on a "peer-to-peer" system, in which each user acted as a node in the infrastructure. That same networking concept underpins TransferWise, the firm that Hinricus and Käärmann launched with their own money in 2011 to enable international money transfers.

The site works by scaling up and automating the initial agreement that the two founders had with each other. Users specify the amount of money they want to send abroad, so let's imagine customer A wants a sum of one thousand dollars to be transferred from the United States to a destination in Britain. At the same time, TransferWise customers in Britain are making similar requests to send money in the other direction. American customers send their money to TransferWise's US account, and British users send their cash to the firm's British account. The firm can then redistribute money from its local account without having to ship it across borders, avoiding fees and the bank's spread on the foreign-exchange transaction.

In the case of customer A, therefore, a sterling amount equivalent to one thousand dollars at the midmarket rate is transferred out of TransferWise's British account and into the account he has specified. Somewhere in the United States, an equivalent transaction is taking place with the money that customer A sent to the start-up's US account. (When there is a temporary imbalance in transfer requests between markets, then the firm still completes the transactions on its own account.) Hinrikus reckons that there is an 85 percent saving on the charges grabbed by the bank in a cross-border transaction.

Customers are finding TransferWise by word of mouth. Although the principal customer base is expatriate professionals, there are plenty of British pensioners living in Spain who use the site to access their retirement income. Businesses are also turning up. The site is gradually building up the list of countries in which it is authorized, with the goal, Hinrikus says, of being able to help people move money internationally wherever they want to send it. There are plans to help online merchants—the sellers of goods on

Amazon, eBay, and so on—use TransferWise to request payments from customers abroad.

Start-ups like TransferWise cannot avoid regulations entirely. Open an account with them, and you'll be asked for all sorts of documentation to meet what are known as "know your customer" requirements, rules that are designed to prevent money laundering. But they can still handily beat the banks for speed: a cross-border "transfer" takes one or two days, compared with up to five for mainstream banks.

FASTER, CHEAPER, SAFER, and more efficient is quite a combination. How worried should the banks be about the new firms, and in particular about lenders like Zopa, Funding Circle, Prosper, and Lending Club? Even the most ardent defenders of peer-to-peer platforms do not think the banks are going to disappear: their processes may be slow, but they can mobilize an awful lot of money and operate across borders to boot. The banks offer a host of services, from payment systems to the simple current account, which makes them very hard to dislodge. Branches still matter in winning business: "Location is still the first and most important decision-maker when you choose your branch" was the verdict of John Stumpf, chairman and chief executive of Wells Fargo, an American bank, in 2012. "After that you might bank online, you might not go back to visit that bank again . . . but that location is where you think your money is."[3]

The fact that savers can access their money instantly also hands banks an enormous advantage. The Lending Club model is predicated on the idea of locking your money up for the duration of the

loan that is being funded. Banks offer depositors an entirely different deal: you can get your cash whenever you want. Even without
the added reassurance of a deposit-guarantee scheme, this ability of
banks to "generate liquidity," in the academic verbiage, is one reason they can fund themselves relatively cheaply despite the amount
of debt that they carry. Laplanche says that the retail money that
goes onto the Lending Club platform comes more from the pot
people use to invest in shares and bonds than from the instant-
access cash they hold in the bank. It will be hard for the new services to fund really long-term loans such as mortgages if it means
lenders cannot get at their money until the borrower pays back. The
very thing that makes banks fragile—maturity transformation—is
also the thing that helps protect them from competition in many
areas. "There will always be a place for insured accounts ensuring
access to liquidity, at expense of yields," acknowledges Laplanche.[4]

The newcomers will force banks to up their game. A recurring
theme in all innovation, not just in finance, is the difficulty that
incumbents have in coming up with new products and services that
are genuinely disruptive. If you are charging a nice spread with your
existing products, the incentive to create another product that earns
you less is rather low. Now that competitors exist, the banks have a
greater incentive to respond—by buying up or launching platforms
of their own. Indeed, it may be that the banks and the newcomers
will end up cooperating as well as competing. Imagine a bank that
doesn't want all of the risk of a small-business loan, perhaps because it is in a region or sector where the lender already has concentrated exposure, but does want to maintain a relationship with the
borrower. It might use a platform like Funding Circle to fund some

of the loan. Lending Club already has partnerships with community banks in the United States in which the banks can buy loans to diversify their loan books.

But the banks also have good reason to be worried by the likes of Laplanche. The banks are being forced by their regulators to reduce leverage, which means they have to find other ways to increase returns to their investors. They could cut costs, but it is hard to imagine they can run leaner ships than the start-ups, which can scale up very efficiently. They could increase the cost of credit, but that simply creates more opportunity for the likes of Lending Club to exploit. The fact that the new platforms are attracting institutional money means that they can start to offer longer-term loans as well as shorter ones; insurers and pension funds are much more prepared to stick their money away for years than other types of investors. And even in a matched-funding model, there is more liquidity than you might think. Borrowers on average pay off loans earlier than their nominal span: the average mortgage in the United States lasts for seven years. And the platforms are slowly developing secondary markets in which their loans can be traded with other investors. Laplanche likes the idea of listing investment funds containing Lending Club loans, for example, so investors can hold shares in the fund and trade it just like equity.

Much will depend, particularly in these early years, on how well the newcomers manage risk. Although they act as marketplaces in which users and suppliers of capital can transact, the platforms cannot just stand back and watch what happens. Remember that a firm like Lending Club has to entice borrowers and savers. It attracts borrowers in part by offering lower rates than the competition and savers by offering higher rates of return than other assets. That balancing act means it has to manage risk and reward tightly. Charge too much, and the borrowers become disinterested. Charge too little, and investors may lose their appetite, or risk being burned by a lot of defaults.

One answer to this problem is to leave things up to investors. The platforms are a marketplace for consenting adults, an opportunity to trust the wisdom of the crowd. Prosper, Lending Club's crosstown rival, started out with this ethos. It used to have an auction system, in which borrowers would specify how much they wanted to pay and lenders would bid to provide them with money. But the crowd is not always wise. A lot of loans did not get funded because borrowers were consistently asking for too low a rate. Lenders were often no better: like other auction sites, Prosper found that there was a small group of people whose goal was to win the auction no matter how low the rate they received as a result.

This sort of foolishness is not just restricted to retail investors. MarketInvoice, an electronic platform in London that allows small firms to sell off their outstanding invoices at a discount, also used to run auctions. Its investors were not members of the public, but high-net-worth individuals, family offices, and specialist funds. Even so, it observed exactly the same kind of behavior, with investors determined to invest their allocation of money no matter what and bidding discounts down to minuscule levels.

Prosper's experiment with an auction system has long since ended. It now assesses borrowers itself and puts them into risk bands that come with a preordained interest rate attached. Lending Club, Zopa, MarketInvoice, and others do the same thing. "Credit is complex and requires analysis that would be too much for individual investors," says Laplanche, whose chief risk officer at Lending Club used to do the same job for JPMorgan Chase's credit-card unit. Such analysis is also often far too much like hard work for institutional investors as well. With very large pots of money to play with, their modus operandi is to specify how much money they want to put into which risk categories, sit back, and watch what happens from afar.

The platforms are also taking on responsibility for making sure that lenders are diversified. A creditor of a big bank trusts that the bank is itself lending across a lot of different sectors and geographies. The bank itself ought to be diversified. If you are lending money directly, then you have to do the work of spreading risk for yourself. In the words of one peer-to-peer backer, "You have to ensure that Granny knows about portfolio theory." So the platforms have developed various tools for automatically parceling investors' money out to different borrowers in different risk categories. Selling loans to investors as securitizations is another way of ensuring diversification.

The upshot is that, in small but significant ways, the platforms are evolving to be more bank-like. The platforms are already doing their own credit analysis. They are already providing diversified portfolios for investors to fund. Some have provisioning funds that, in effect, mimic the role of equity by protecting lenders from defaults. RateSetter, one of the British platforms, is even carrying out a mild version of maturity transformation by allowing investors to loan money for shorter periods than the loans that are being funded. Some in the industry already float the possibility of having a current account attached to their lending platforms, perhaps even of having deposit insurance extended to them.

With such responsibility comes risk. As the peer-to-peer platforms take on some of the roles of a normal bank, they can expect to suffer more if borrowers default in greater than expected numbers. Although they are not financial intermediaries, the platforms will still lose the confidence of investors. As Laplanche says, "The subprime-mortgage crisis stemmed from a long chain of people, with diffuse responsibility for decisions. We originate, underwrite, price, and service. If loans don't perform, it is on us."

To obviate this risk, the platforms therefore have a strong incentive to concentrate on the most creditworthy, or "prime," borrowers. Lending Club, for example, goes after borrowers with a FICO credit score above 600, the technical definition of prime, which cuts its addressable market down from $850 billion of outstanding credit-card debt to (a mere) $300 billion. When I met its founders, Funding Circle screened out small businesses that had been borrowing for less than two years; its borrowers typically had an annual turnover of £600,000 and above, had a staff of eight employees, and had been trading for more than ten years. CommonBond has deliberately concentrated on graduates and MBA students in high-earning subjects from well-regarded colleges.

The issue for these businesses is whether they can continue to grow without compromising on the features that make them successful, and on risk management in particular. For now, the ceiling on growth seems a long way off. But the temptation to dial risk up a notch without properly charging for it will test the peer-to-peer platforms eventually, as it does everyone in finance. The industry failed that test spectacularly during the subprime-mortgage boom. The question that preoccupies our next category of financial entrepreneurs is whether it is possible to do a better job of serving less creditworthy borrowers.

CHAPTER 8

THE EDGE:
REACHING THE
MARGINAL BORROWER

Douglas Merrill is typical of a new breed of entrepreneurs with the financial industry in their sights. He does not have a financial background. His expertise is in computer science and mathematics: in a prior life, he was the chief information officer for Google. He preaches the gospel of "big data," the use of the enormous amounts of digital data now stored on all of us, to improve the way that business is done. He is based not in the financial centers on America's East Coast, but in Los Angeles. And the firm he founded, ZestFinance, came about because Merrill saw personally how finance was failing ordinary people.

That moment came when he was called by his sister-in-law, who was telephoning because she needed money to fix a flat tire. Merrill helped her out, but asked her later what she would have done if he hadn't been around to pick up the phone. Her answer was that she would have gone to a payday lender. By that stage he had already left Google and was looking for a new problem to get his teeth into. Payday lending seemed to fit the bill perfectly.

It is a very large industry: there are twenty-four thousand payday outlets in the United States, compared with a little more than fourteen thousand McDonald's restaurants in 2012. A survey by the Federal Deposit Insurance Corporation found that roughly one in twelve American households, or some 17 million adults, are "unbanked," meaning they lack a current account; another one in every five households has an account but uses alternatives as well—payday loans, check-cashing services, pawn shops, and the like.[1]

A lot of guff is talked about the evils of payday lending. When people have a need for cash, it is generally better for them to go to actual businesses with physical outlets than to turn to loan sharks with baseball bats. Although predatory lenders undoubtedly exist, the deeper problem is that even the good ones end up charging high rates of interest in order to cover not just their operating costs, but also the higher credit risks that they are taking on by making unsecured loans to low-income borrowers. That can easily turn a short-term loan to cover a cash shortfall into a chronic debt problem. A survey by the Consumer Financial Protection Bureau in 2013 found that nearly half of payday borrowers have more than ten transactions a year and that 14 percent borrow twenty or more times annually. Payday borrowers are indebted a median of 199 days in the year.

Merrill saw this as an opportunity that he was well qualified to address. "People do not know how to underwrite," he says. "They cannot figure out whether people can pay back, so they assume no one will and price very high accordingly. This is a maths problem." ZestFinance was founded to improve the quality of underwriting so that payday lenders did not have to charge as much.

Perhaps the most used technique in credit scoring is something called "logistic regression." This is a technique used to predict the probability that a loan will go sour by tracing the relationships that exist between certain "independent variables" such as age or income, say, and the eventual payment outcome (the "dependent variable"). Normally, this technique uses a smallish number of independent variables to assess the chances that a borrower will default—perhaps as few as ten bits of data. That causes trouble when one of those pieces is missing, something that is more likely to happen with people who are outside the formal banking system. Suddenly, the model is left scrambling for sufficient information to be able to make its prediction. One option is to assume a value for the missing bit of data and still let the model whir. But when credit risks are already high, the incentives for payday lenders are skewed toward either rejecting someone's application altogether or jacking up interest rates even further.

Merrill thinks that the answer is to find more and more data. Using cookies to track how carefully someone is reading the firm's terms and conditions is one variable to look at as a sign of how seriously a would-be borrower is taking things. Tying bits of data together is vital, too. Repeated changes in cell-phone numbers might indicate a serial defaulter on phone contracts or it might mean someone who moves a lot for seasonal work and is changing numbers. Joining the dots between phone numbers and postal addresses can provide that vital extra bit of context.

By scouring the Internet and databases for information on applicants, the ZestFinance underwriting model draws on up to ten thousand variables, which between them generate seventy thousand "signals." Each of these signals is looked at by ten machine-learning models that take a slightly different view of creditworthiness: one might look at probability of default, another at the chances of collecting on unpaid debts, and so on. Finally, all of these perspectives are "ensembled," a high-powered form of smooshing, into a final score that can then be used to make a lending decision.

These thousands of variables are not all equally important, of course. But using a lot of them means the model can survive the omission of individual pieces of data—no single one is vital. The same goes for inaccuracies: a surprising number of applicants apparently show up as dead in official records. Underpinning this much larger data set is the belief that even information that looks entirely irrelevant to creditworthiness has something to tell lenders. ZestFinance has found, for example, that there are slight differences in the payment outcomes of people who type their names differently (that is, between those who use capitals for the initial letters and then lowercase letters, those who write their names out entirely in uppercase, and those who just use lowercase). People who write their names out in capitals for the initial letters and then lowercase turn out to be more creditworthy. Merrill speculates that these are the sort of people who follow the rules when they do not have to. Such relationships are the kind that the firm's algorithms can draw out.

Douglas Merrill is not the only one trying to find new ways to serve the people that the mainstream financial industry marginalizes. Wonga is a British firm that also uses data to extend loans fast. It is controversial—in 2013 the firm was sucked into an improbable row about payday lending involving the archbishop of Canterbury—but it has been growing remarkably fast. It posted profits of £40 million in 2013.

Prepaid cards, which consumers can load up with money and then use for purchases without needing a bank account, are another growth area. The Mercator Advisory Group forecasts the total dollar amount that Americans will load onto these cards in 2015 will be around $390 billion, more than ten times as much as in 2006. The concept of "microfinance," which means providing financial services on a small scale to the poor, was pioneered by a Bangladeshi lender called Grameen Bank, which started out in the 1970s by providing small loans to women in a village called Jobra. Its founder (and Nobel peace laureate), Muhammad Yunus, has now brought Grameen to the United States.[2]

The environment for these kinds of ventures has become more fertile since the 2007–2008 crisis. The marginalized in society have always found it hard to gain access to mainstream finance. But things have gotten worse in recent years. That is partly because there are more people in financial difficulty and partly because of the stigma associated with serving the subprime segment of the market. But it is also because of the harsher regulatory climate for financial institutions.

In the United States the 2009 Credit Card Accountability, Responsibility, and Disclosure (Credit CARD) Act reduced interest-rate increases and late fees on credit cards. The Consumer Financial Protection Bureau is looking at overdraft fees and the prepaid-cards market. The Durbin Amendment—passed as part of the Dodd-Frank Act in July 2010—capped interchange fees, the commission that merchants pay, on debit cards. Add in persistently low interest rates, which have eaten into banks' net interest margins, and Oliver Wyman, a consultancy, has estimated that US banks lose money on 37 percent of consumer accounts. The rich will still pay their way in this sort of environment, thanks to larger account balances and the prospect of higher-margin activities such as investment advice. But the economics of banking the poor is far less attractive than it was.

And, of course, there is the hangover from the housing crisis. Just as entrepreneurs could use their houses as collateral to fund their businesses, the poor could use housing to gain access to credit. According to the Federal Reserve Bank of New York, between 1999 and the end of the third quarter of 2008, when Lehman Brothers imploded, American consumers went from owing their creditors $4.6 trillion to owing them $12.7 trillion. Mortgages and home equity lines of credit accounted for $6.7 trillion of this increase.[3]

Money washed toward less creditworthy borrowers in particular. An analysis by Atif Mian and Amir Sufi of the University of Chicago looked at the flow of mortgage credit by ZIP code. By identifying the fraction of mortgage applicants that had been denied mortgages in a particular ZIP code in 1996, and then looking at the experience of the same ZIP code in 2001–2005, they found that credit flowed disproportionately to areas where previously applications had been denied—despite the fact that these areas suffered lower income and employment growth than others. Mortgage growth was driven by the less creditworthy borrower.[4]

Once in their homes, households could unlock yet more credit by borrowing against the equity. A 2013 study by the Federal Reserve Bank of New York showed that on average for every 1 percent rise in house prices, home owners increased their mortgage debt by 1 percent. As fast as the value of their equity rose, home owners turned it into debt.[5]

All that has changed. Mortgages and equity withdrawal are no longer the freely available options they once were. Other forms of credit (except for student loans) are also constrained. Between September 2008 and September 2012, American household debt dropped by 11 percent, to $11.3 trillion, partly because of write-offs, partly because of greater saving, and partly because of tighter credit standards. The effect is to leave lower-income members of society with fewer options.

MERRILL'S VENTURE AND other attempts to funnel money to borrowers that banks do not often reach raise a really big question about finance as a whole. How should credit get to marginal borrowers, those people right on the edge of the financial system? The precrisis answer to this question was basically to dodge it. Lending to the poor through the housing channel enabled banks to make a bet on the collateral, rather than on the person. As long as house prices kept rising, the logic ran, a borrower in distress could refinance or sell out. In the event of default and repossession, the bank could hope to make enough money on the sale of the property to wash its face.

To be clear, the likes of ZestFinance and Wonga are not reprising the subprime-mortgage boom. They are in the business of unsecured lending. They cannot rely on collateral to provide a safety net. The financial chemistry is more stable, too: mortgages are long-term loans, and these are short-term ones. These types of lender do not take retail deposits to fund themselves. And the goals are different as well: where subprime mortgages promised to transform people's quality of living, Merrill has a more modest one of maintaining it. But there is nonetheless an echo of what went on in the mortgage industry—namely, the industrialization of credit, as the crunching of data enables lenders to make rapid decisions on risky borrowers without so much as a handshake.

That bothers a lot of people. Many critics of banks look wistfully back to a golden age of finance, when the bank manager was the gateway to credit, when judgment prevailed over equation-filled models. This was a world of conservatism and integrity, where taxpayers slept easy in their beds and bankers were more Jimmy Stewart than Gordon Gekko. Since then, modern finance has evolved toward replacing decentralized judgment by mechanical process and substituting relationship lending with arms-length transactions. You can apply for loans online in minutes without speaking to anyone. Thanks to securitization, your mortgage may no longer be owned by the bank you got it from. The risks associated with extending your mortgage can be hedged on the basis of mathematical formulas.[6]

At first glance, it looks hard to argue against a relationship-based approach to lending. The better a bank knows a borrower, surely the more likely it is to make a decent credit decision in the first place and maintain a constructive partnership afterward. One example that people point to is an enviably successful Swedish bank called Svenska Handelsbanken. Handelsbanken sailed through the financial crisis with a model founded on what it calls the "church-tower principle," the idea that branch managers should do business only as far as they can see from the local spire. Decision making is extremely decentralized; the branches make all the credit decisions, and there are no detailed budget targets for them to meet. Customers do not spend years of their lives waiting in call-center lines; they call up and speak to a person whose name they know. There is no bonus culture, either. If Handelsbanken's return-on-equity goals are met, then a portion of the profits is funneled into the bank's pension scheme, which is its largest shareholder. It's all wonderfully Swedish.

But personalized service and relationship banking are also expensive. The Handelsbanken model works because it is selective about the types of customers it takes on. The bank itself acknowledges that a mass-market bank would find it tough to copy its model and be profitable.

And there are dangers to human interaction as well as to models. Anil Stocker is a cofounder of MarketInvoice, the British platform on which small businesses can sell their unpaid invoices to investors at a discount; the firm had processed close to £300 million in funding by late 2014. Unlike factoring, in which small firms sell all their invoices to a single provider, Stocker's business enables firms to sell individual invoices and fractions of invoices. The firms get cash quicker than they otherwise would, and the investors get a return when the invoices are paid. Youthful, fidgety, and impressive, Stocker is a onetime employee of Lehman Brothers and a first-time entrepreneur. Although the ultimate payer of the invoice is someone else, it is vital to Stocker's business that he correctly assesses the risk of the small business that is selling the invoice. It is when that business goes bust that an invoice is less likely to be paid. He will not allow his risk team to meet small businesses face-to-face; he wants them to be screened on the basis of hard data, not soft indicators. "You start listening to their story—and they all have a story," he says, with the conviction of a man who has been too trusting in the past. It is an argument echoed by Errol Damelin, the founder of Wonga: "Do not believe the bank line that they are well placed to make credit judgments. Humans are not good at the anecdotal, impressionistic judgment."

Relying on relationships can be bad for borrowers as well as lenders. An analysis of overdrafts in Italy found that credit lines given by banks to self-employed women and very small firms owned by women systematically charge a higher interest rate than those given to businesses owned by men. The higher interest rate has nothing to do with the creditworthiness of the business. Indeed, firms owned by women have a lower failure rate than those owned by men. It gets worse. When a borrower is asked for a guarantor, that reflects a higher perception of risk and leads to a higher interest rate on average. But an Italian woman with a male guarantor finds that her interest rate goes down, not up. A woman guaranteed by another woman is seen by banks as the worst client of all, a toxic accumulation of dizzy-minded risks. It is hard to look at this indictment of a traditional banking system and conclude that a machine would do things worse.[7]

BIG DATA IS NOT the only thing coming to the aid of poorer people. Behavioral finance, the use of psychological insights to understand how people interact with money, is also helping. Like a firm, every person has a capital structure, comprising the amount of credit they borrow and the amount of equity they can call on. The two are intimately related: the more of their own cash they have, the less likely they are to have to turn to payday lenders. But huge chunks of the population are operating without any cushion to protect them against unexpected outlays. This is the problem that Douglas Merrill's sister had when she needed to change her tire. A 2012 survey of Americans' personal finances asked how confident respondents were that they could come up with $2,000 if an unexpected need arose; almost 40 percent of Americans could not or probably could not come up with that amount of money if they needed to. Almost two-thirds of respondents did not have three months of emergency funds that they could access to cover expenses in the event of sickness or job loss.[8]

The answer to this problem is screamingly obvious: people need to save more. But getting them to do so is clearly very hard: even people with decent incomes routinely fail to put aside enough money. Hence the growing interest in using behavioral nudges, of the kind that encourage people to put more money into their pensions scheme, to encourage more saving among lower-income households. One idea is to use the power of social incentives to encourage people to save, by translating a very old idea from the analog world to the digital world. The very old idea is that of a Rotating Savings and Credit Association, or ROSCA, a group of people who band together in order to save and borrow. Each member of the club puts in a small amount of money every time it meets, and each person in the group is chosen at random to receive the whole savings pot once during the lifetime of the association. If ten people agree to each set aside $20 a week, over a period of ten weeks each will win $200 dollars at some point. The advantages of the system are partly mathematical: a group member reaches his or her savings goal twice as fast on average as they would do on their own. But they are also behavioral: the power of social ties means that default rates (that is, on the public commitment to keep saving even if you have already taken home the weekly pool) are very low.

ROSCAs work very well in emerging markets: they are extremely common in markets where banking systems are undeveloped and cash is king. But they may have a high-tech future as well. A Silicon Valley start-up called ClearStreet wants to take the model online, with an app that allows people to join a digital savings circle in which members make the same sorts of commitments to save into a common pool. The challenge will be to replicate the power of real-world relationships in a virtual environment. The social cost of defaulting on people who live in the same village is clearly greater than the cost of defaulting on strangers. Kim Polese, who was the original product manager for Java and counts as bona fide Silicon Valley royalty, is the chairwoman of ClearStreet. She acknowledges the problem. Her plan is to begin by moving existing social connections online. Faith-based organizations, whose worshippers already belong to a community, are an obvious starting point for testing whether social circles can exist digitally.

From a small office in the center of San Francisco, Rod Ebrahimi and Ignacio Thayer are also harnessing behavioral insights to help people manage their finances. Ready for Zero is a start-up that allows consumers to link up all of their financial accounts and helps them set a target for reducing their debts. The business began, like so many start-ups, from a personal problem that mainstream finance was not addressing properly. Ebrahimi's girlfriend had racked up thousands in student debt and asked for his advice on how to go about paying it down. A jerrybuilt spreadsheet was the initial answer to that request, but Ebrahimi, whose background was in cloud computing, and Thayer, another former Google employee, realized that there was a bigger opportunity. Student debt is over $1 trillion of outstanding loans. Some 70 percent of households in the United States have at least one credit card, and in 2010 more than half of these households carried an average of $12,900 of interest-bearing debt over from one month to the next, at a cost of more than $140 per month.[9]

Ready for Zero shows how much money consumers owe across their credit cards, student-loan balances, and other obligations and constructs a personal payment plan to get their debts down. The technology and the math that underlie the site are impressive, but the business's real proposition is behavioral. By setting up payments to come out of accounts automatically, the problem of inertia is overcome. Notifications that prompt people to pay off more debt when they get lump sums into their accounts are designed to help deal with the problem of hyperbolic discounting, which in this context is the tendency for people who want to pay down debt to blow through their paycheck in the week they get paid. A bar that shows progress toward repayment goals offers a simple visual cue to encourage good behavior: Thayer emphasizes its importance in motivating users. (Robert Merton's SmartNest, the product we encountered in Chapter 5, also uses visualization to convey how people are getting on: it features a speedometer graphic to convey the probability of hitting your targeted retirement income.)

Another behavioral lever that can be pulled in order to increase savings is the dangling of prizes as a reward for putting money aside. Humans love lotteries. In the year 2008, forty-two states in the United States and the District of Columbia offered state lotteries, bringing in roughly $60 billion in sales, or more than $540 per household nationwide. In the same year, American households spent $430 each on all dairy products and $444 on alcohol. Some of this lottery fever is explained by the element of suspense, which adds excitement. Some of it is explained by our inability to calculate probabilities well. For poorer consumers in particular, a lottery may seem like the most realistic, and certainly the fairest, avenue to a windfall. The introduction of state lotteries in the United States is associated with a 3 percent reduction of non-gambling-related expenditures by low-income households.[10]

The question is whether this love of lotteries can be harnessed for constructive purposes. The introduction of limited liability for equity investors in the nineteenth century—which means that shareholders can lose no more than the money they used to buy the stock—is an example of how the lottery impulse can be redirected. Limited liability was a vital step in the development of modern equity markets for other reasons, too, but the possibility of "winning" a jackpot many times larger than their original stake without having to worry about an equivalent downside helped foster public acceptance of stock-market investing. The same instincts can also be used to encourage more saving.[11]

Peter Tufano is a former Harvard Business School academic who is now the dean of the Said Business School in Oxford. As well as writing about financial innovation, he is also a practitioner. Tufano's particular concern has been how to encourage the poor to increase their savings. The low-income consumer is a market that holds little allure for the banks. Families with incomes of $10,000 or so are not going to be taking out mortgages or investing in equities, which is how lenders make serious money.

In 2000 Tufano founded a Boston-based nonprofit organization called the Doorways to Dreams (D2D) Fund that was designed to experiment with ways to encourage the poor to save. As well as marshaling behavioral insights about the need to make saving seem attractive, Tufano also realized that the same problems that turn the banks off marginal customers—not enough revenue for the costs involved—would need to be solved by any new product. In particular, the trick would be keeping customer-acquisition costs down. Tufano and his colleagues saw a potential solution in the huge natural demand for lotteries. By offering prizes to people who saved, the customers should come to them.

The idea of prize-linked savings is not new. A craze for lotteries swept England back in the 1690s, for example, and the government was quick to harness their potential. The Million Adventure was a lottery organized in 1694 to help fund the government's military expenditure: it offered one hundred thousand tickets for a cost of £10 each, of which twenty-five hundred would yield prizes ranging from a payment of £10 a year for sixteen years to £1,000 a year over that period. The Million Adventure was also a savings initiative: it paid ticket holders an interest payment of £1 each year until 1710. Although £10 was a handsome sum of money, syndicates formed to enable people with lower incomes to club together to buy tickets; the lottery is reckoned to have attracted tens of thousands of participants in this way.[12]

Prize-linked savings schemes remain common today, at least outside the United States. Commercial lenders in Latin America offer prize-linked accounts; Sweden's debt office issues lottery bonds where investors forgo interest payments but can win prizes instead; Britain's "Premium Bonds" give savers a unique number for every £1 they invest, each one of which is a chance to win in a monthly prize drawing.

Tufano and his colleagues believed that this sort of scheme ought to be tried in the United States, too. In 2009 the D2D Fund launched a prize-linked savings product in Michigan (one of the few places where private lotteries are not banned). Called Save to Win, the product is distributed by credit unions, a type of financial cooperative, and offers both annual prizes and smaller monthly ones so that savers have frequent chances to win. A saver earns raffle tickets for every $25 deposited in the account, with a cap of ten entries per month. Versions of the same product have been introduced in Nebraska, South Carolina, and Washington. The hope is that D2D can eventually tap into the state-lottery system itself in order to distribute the product. More than fifty thousand members have saved over $94 million since the scheme was launched. That might not sound like much, but for low-income families "much" is a relative concept; insiders say the evidence suggests that these are new savings.

PEOPLE ARE NOT the only marginal borrowers. Like individuals who lack a decent credit history, small businesses are often short of the data that make them easy to analyze. They also tend to be more vulnerable to financial shocks, which gives lenders another reason to steer clear. And because their borrowing requirements are relatively small, they fly beneath the radar of institutional investors that have credit-assessment capabilities but want to put their money to work only in hefty chunks. That ought to make them perfect fodder for the banks. What other institutions have a physical infrastructure that reaches into local communities and the expertise to analyze creditworthiness? Yet no one seems that happy with the service that the banks provide. The problems that small businesses have in financing themselves predated the 2007–2008 crisis. Banks have a large cost base and will always find it more cost-effective to make a $1 million loan than a $50,000 one. Banks are keen on collateral, and many businesses do not have security to offer. In the past they could have used their home equity, but that is no longer an option. Because small-business owners often start out using personal borrowing to fund their enterprises, by the time they need to borrow from the banks, their own credit scores have dropped and the lenders run shy.

Since the crisis, things have gotten a lot worse. In a period of risk aversion, the incentive is for lenders to concentrate on larger firms or customers with collateral. When capital rules are hardening, it makes sense to direct lending to activities where the capital charges are less onerous, which means mortgages rather than small businesses. The problem of banks pulling back on lending is particularly bad in Europe, where they dominate the provision of credit, accounting for an estimated 80 percent of financing before the crisis. To this problem of scarcity, the data mavens have a familiar answer. By scraping information from all sorts of sources, they reckon they can build an accurate real-time sense of the health of a small business. OnDeck (formerly OnDeck Capital) is a New York–based firm that was founded in 2007 and takes as little as a few minutes to extend loans to small firms. It strongly rejects the "whites-of-the-eyes" banking model. "That often reflects a different view of the world," says Noah Breslow, the firm's chief executive. "It is made by people who think you should lend because you know their brothers-in-law, not because of data." OnDeck asks potential borrowers to fill out an online form to apply for funds and then quickly gathers information from all over the place: not just the usual personal and corporate-credit scores, but also online banking transactions and balances, payments to vendors, and public records like public-health ratings for restaurants. Like ZestFinance, it isn't just looking at absolute values but also examining the rate of change in numbers, in order to provide a sense of the business's growth trajectory.

OnDeck lends only to businesses that have been operating for a year or more—younger than that and the data trail is too short. But it still has to be able to sniff out faint data footprints, especially if this is a newish firm applying for credit for the first time. Social media can be helpful at the margins: a restaurant with eighty Yelp reviews is clearly doing business, but one with only three reviews may not be. Assessments get easier as the firm's scoring algorithms get smarter. OnDeck's model spots clustering in the data to gauge patterns of creditworthiness, a bit like Amazon's recommendations algorithm spotting what groups of things buyers put in their on-line baskets. It also uses machine learning to improve its classifica-tions. Standard credit bureaus might classify an auto-repair shop in the same industry as a car dealership, for example. Since OnDeck would be much keener to loan money to a body shop than to a dealership, the model is trained to make finer judgments based on things like the name of the firm. The big banks have woken up to the potential of this approach: they are already using OnDeck's scoring model to take a second look at borrowers they feel unsure about.

Just as OnDeck can make loan-application decisions quickly, the firm can also be faster to react to changes in the circumstances of existing borrowers. It uses a micropayment model, in which pay-ments are taken automatically every business day from borrowers' accounts. Breslow claims that the businesses do not mind: avoid-ing lumpy payments at the end of the month is actually a bene-fit. What's more, it means that OnDeck can see if someone is in trouble early on. He cites the example of a pizza restaurant located in a town that was dominated by two employers: a manufacturer and a university. The manufacturer went bust in the summer, but OnDeck was able quickly to restructure the debt until the univer-sity term started again and the students returned to tuck into pizza again.

Anil Stocker is similarly evangelical about the ability of his business to spot trouble via data: one of the things that Market-Invoice looks for is directors leaving their firms, since there is an incentive for directors of struggling firms to deregister in a bid to avoid any liability in the event of failure. Where there is data, of course, privacy concerns also arise: the risk chief at another new lender talks wistfully of how nice it would be to know whether directors' marriages are stable, since trouble at home can be an indicator of trouble at work. Neither OnDeck nor MarketInvoice is the cheapest source of capital, but availability, speed, and convenience often count for more than price. That is also the business case behind Kabbage, a data-driven online lender that is based in Atlanta, Georgia, and specializes in providing working capital to the merchants who sell goods on online platforms like Amazon and eBay. If a merchant can get hold of an advance quickly and turn that quickly into a return, then paying a bit more can be a reasonable decision. What businesses do not want is a lot of paperwork and a rejection at the end of it—a "slow no," in the jargon.

Like its rivals, Kabbage is plumbing new data sources to assess the state of its borrowers' businesses. It has a partnership with UPS, for example, that allows loan applicants to enable Kabbage to see the amount of goods that they ship; even information on things like box size can be a useful proxy for risk. The firm has struck a similar agreement with Intuit that allows it to gain permitted access to small businesses' data on QuickBooks, an accounting program. Like the dabs on a pointillist painting, each bit of data creates a more powerful overall impression. Kabbage can process an application from a seller of goods on eBay and within minutes see how actively the merchant uses UPS and how many deals it tweets a week, gauge trends in website traffic from Google Trends, and look at its accounts via QuickBooks. "Data context is the secret sauce," says Marc Gorlin, Kabbage's chairman. "This is not so much about points in time, more about the spaces in between. If I can see from the payroll data that two firms each have ten employees, but one had twenty a month ago and the other five, then one is obviously better placed than the other." Any model can spit out bad answers, of course, but this feels nothing like the simple lending heuristics of the subprime boom.

The arena of alternative finance for small business is only going to become more crowded. Firms like PayPal and Amazon are already extending credit to the merchants that use their platforms. China's equivalent to Amazon, Alibaba.com, is doing the same—in a country where the large state-owned banks have disproportionately directed credit to state-owned enterprises, that has the potential to be transformative. Breslow's vision of the future is more radical still. "We want eventually to get to the point where you don't apply for credit at all. Instead, you would go to a bank's site or to a point-of-sale page and see that you have credit available to you, and just click on it."

The subprime crisis has tarnished the idea of serving less creditworthy borrowers. But getting credit to people and businesses that are walled off from it is exactly the sort of challenge with which financial entrepreneurs ought to be grappling. Solving the problem of the marginal borrower is below the radar of many mainstream institutions; it is also susceptible to the application of new technology and behavioral insights. As we saw in Chapter 2, however, innovative thinking can over time lead to very bad outcomes. Markets get bigger, people become complacent, and risks grow until they can overwhelm the system as a whole. The next and final chapter looks at how finance can do better at managing very big risks, including the ones it generates itself.

CHAPTER 9

TAIL RISK:
PRICING THE
PROBABILITY OF MAYHEM

As job titles go, Gordon Woo's takes some beating. Woo is a catastrophist, and his job is to think about tail risks—the sorts of big risks that occur outside the normal distribution of events and lurk in the long tails of probability. To be more precise, his job is to think about disasters. Earthquakes, hurricanes, terrorist attacks, and pandemics are his raw materials; models that calculate the probability of catastrophes and the damage they might cause are the products he helps to turn out.

Woo is a physicist by background and an academic by temperament and appearance. His is a macabre world. Woo was behind a risk model that worked out the probability of a large-scale terrorist attack on the 2006 World Cup in Germany. FIFA, the world's governing body for soccer (football), wanted to take out insurance against the event being canceled; just about the only thing that could plausibly lead to the whole tournament being called off was a terrorist atrocity. Woo's job was to quantify just how probable that was.

Among other things, that meant methodically working out the probabilities of a detonation of a nuclear device by a terrorist organization. The bad news is that Woo has no doubt at all about the willingness of terrorists to deploy a weapon of this sort. The good news is that he assumes a plan to acquire and deploy a nuclear bomb would require a lot of people working in concert, making it more likely that the intelligence agencies would detect them.

Woo's job requires him to think about almost every conceivable disaster. We first met a few days after a meteorite had entered the earth's atmosphere over Russia and exploded in the air above the region of Chelyabinsk, injuring as many as fifteen hundred people. The Chelyabinsk object was the largest to have entered our atmosphere since a 1908 meteorite known as the Tunguska event, which also struck Russia and flattened an estimated 80 million trees. The chances of a meteorite striking Germany was another thing Woo considered in designing the World Cup risk model, but this was one he ended up dismissing. Some probabilities (like that of England winning the tournament) are just too low to assess properly.[1]

Woo works at a firm called Risk Management Solutions (RMS), one of three large companies (the others are AIR Worldwide and Eqecat) that specialize in modeling catastrophes. Such firms are a vital cog in a young market for "insurance-linked securities," financial products that help insurers and reinsurers share the risk of really big claims with the fund managers who look after the world's biggest pots of money.

Natural catastrophes are the industry's bread and butter. There are models that calculate the hazard of earthquakes occurring in Tokyo, of hurricanes making land in Florida, and of hailstorms battering cars in Europe. As well as working out how likely it is that an event of a certain magnitude will happen, the models also calculate how big a bill it would hand to insurers.

Until the late 1980s, the losses caused by natural catastrophes were not an issue on insurers' radars. They had been lulled by the recent past, and in particular by a strangely calm period in the 1970s and 1980s, when there were pretty much no natural catastrophes that caused large-scale insured damage in developed economies. A world without disasters was seen as the norm.

That perception began to change with Hurricane Hugo, which hit America's Eastern Seaboard in 1989. But the real shock to the system was Hurricane Andrew, which blew through Florida and other southern states in 1992, causing estimated damage of $23 billion. The insurance industry's capacity to meet claims was severely tested. Several insurers ended up filing for bankruptcy, and the strategy of relying on the resources of reinsurers, the firms that insure the insurers, looked flimsier than many had supposed.

Think of this strategy as being a bit like a champagne tower, the big pyramid of champagne glasses you get on cruises and at showy weddings. Losses first accumulate at the top of the pyramid, which is where the policyholder sits. Home owners whose properties have been ruined by an earthquake, say, will retain some of these losses in the form of a policy excess. The rest of the claims will spill over to the next level, the insurers. These insurers will retain some of the losses but do not want to expose themselves to all of the risk of a big event. So they shed some of the risk by letting losses above a certain magnitude cascade down to the next set of players, the reinsurance firms.

What Hurricane Andrew showed was that losses could be big enough to overwhelm the reinsurers, too. What was needed was another level of the champagne tower to hold losses beyond a certain scale. And what that meant was finding a way to share risk with the biggest pool of money there is, the capital markets.

The answer is the catastrophe bond. The basic concept is very simple. A reinsurer or an insurer issues a bond to investors. The money they invest gets tucked away into safe assets like government debt. Investors get a coupon (an interest payment), and at the end of the term of the bond (anywhere from three to five years, typically) they get their money back, but only if there hasn't been a natural catastrophe that triggers payment of the cash to the issuer. If there has been a triggering event, however, the money is released to the catastrophe bond issuer, and losses flow down to the investors, the next level of the tower.[2]

Whether the reinsurance industry has the capacity to cope with a large claim is not the immediate priority when a natural disaster occurs, of course. Then the attention is on rescuing and caring for survivors. But once the world has moved on and the long job of rebuilding lives and livelihoods is under way, the point of insurance is to make a bad situation more tolerable. A 2012 analysis by researchers at the Bank for International Settlements showed just how important it is to an economy to have insurance when a disaster strikes. By analyzing growth in the wake of 2,476 natural catastrophes across more than two hundred countries between

1960 and 2011, the researchers found that well-insured catastrophes have inconsequential medium-term effects on growth, or even positive ones, as insurance claims help to fund reconstruction. It is a very different story when there is no insurance, however: uninsured losses result in a cumulative median drop in economic output of almost 2 percent in a "typical" catastrophe.[3]

If insurance matters, then the industry's capacity to cover losses must do so, too. That capacity is being strained as the amount of property at risk in vulnerable areas rises. People keep flocking to Florida despite the hurricanes: an average of one thousand new residents relocated to the Sunshine State every day between 1950 and 2010. The Miami hurricane of 1926 caused $1 billion worth of damage in current dollars. Today it would cause insured losses of $125 billion, according to AIR Worldwide. The damage from another Hurricane Andrew would now be twice what it was then.[4]

It is a similar story in other, less developed, markets. The concentration of property on China's coasts is only going to increase. The globalization of supply chains means that big losses can increasingly occur in unlikely areas: one of the biggest loss events of 2011 was flooding in Thailand, which inundated a series of industrial parks used by electronics and car manufacturers. Total claims for that disaster were estimated at $12 billion, a figure that took many insurers by surprise. The long-run trend for losses from disasters slopes upward.

The amount of cat bonds outstanding now totals around $20 billion. A number that only ends in billion is chicken feed compared with a lot of other financial assets. The size of the global market for debt securities (that is, bonds, not loans), for instance, was estimated by the Bank for International Settlements at $78 trillion in 2012. But there are two reasons to look at the development of this relatively young asset class and cheer. The first is that it performs a genuinely useful function, transferring risk from institutions that lack the capacity to hold it to those that do have such capacity. That may sound ominously familiar: the idea of spreading risk from the banks to the capital markets through the process of mortgage securitization was widely applauded in the run-up to the 2007–2008 crisis. But this is a genuine risk-transfer instrument: if they are triggered, investors really aren't getting their money back.

The second is that the market has some built-in safeguards against runaway growth. Growth is not a bad thing. But out-of-control growth usually has an unhealthy effect on pricing. This is true across financial markets, from mortgage-backed securities before the bust to high-yield bonds in the years succeeding it. Mispriced risk could lead to a nasty surprise for investors in the event of a really big natural disaster—the $100–$200 billion catastrophe that has yet to strike but could if, for example, a big earthquake struck a major city directly.

Nonetheless, the market is unlikely to grow too big too quickly. If markets are to get really big, they need a lot of demand *and* a lot of supply. Catastrophe risk is not a market for people who want to take speculative bets. It is an area where there is decent transparency about the probabilities of a disaster occurring but no transparency about timing. Even if you thought it was worth paying the premiums to get a payout on a disaster, you might have to wait a hundred years to be proved right. So growth will depend on the actual needs of insurers and reinsurers: you wouldn't issue a cat bond for an earthquake unless you wanted to hedge the risk of said earthquake occurring. Although insured values are growing, a stampede to issue is unlikely, and that means there is less chance of the quality of analysis being compromised in the rush to get things done.

THERE IS ANOTHER REASON to like the cat-bond industry: the modeling that underpins it. In a world devoted to calculating the risk of the next natural catastrophe, no one ever gets complacent or comfortable. "The big beast is always out there," says Gordon Woo cheerfully. That means designing models that dive deeply into the historical records for guidance. The very long view can turn up some surprising risks: a tsunami caused by a massive rockfall at the other end of the lake devastated the spot now occupied by Geneva in AD 536.[5]

Looking back at the past is not enough, however. By definition, the worst disaster ever was unprecedented at the time. Woo argues that you need to dive inside the structural causes of catastrophe to understand how things that haven't happened before might unfold in the future. He has been involved in modeling the risk of an earthquake in Monaco, for example, even though there have been no losses in this spot in the past. Insurers still want to know what the probabilities of a quake would be. Monaco has an enormous concentration of very expensive property, and it is built on slopes, so if one house goes it may well start a cascade of other collapses. By looking at all possible earthquake epicenters and all plausible magnitudes, Woo could come up with an answer. He thinks this kind of approach—imagining the ways in which the worst can happen—could be applied to finance itself. During the run-up to the 2007–2008 crisis, for example, the catastrophic risk the financial system faced was a national housing bust in the United States. Most financial models dismissed this risk: they looked at recent data that showed the potential for regional housing downturns but nothing countrywide. Someone like Woo, in contrast, would not have cared how long it had been since the last national downturn, or even if there had been one. His concern would have been to understand how a housing crash might come about and how bad it might get.

To understand the steps that Woo takes in more detail, let's turn from natural disasters to another kind of "peak risk"—the risk of a lethal pandemic. Peak risks are what they sound like: sudden events that cause a spike in losses big enough to threaten the capacity of insurance firms and of the reinsurers that stand behind them. A pandemic would certainly fit into that category.

Working out the probability and likely impact of a pandemic looks like a fool's errand. Natural catastrophes may seem random, but they are at least sufficiently regular that the models can draw on a lot of historical data. By contrast, the world hasn't suffered a really lethal pandemic since the "Spanish flu" of 1918–1919, which killed an estimated 40–50 million people in little more than a year. Disasters like earthquakes unfold very quickly in comparison with pandemics; that additional time increases the number of potential paths the disease might take. And whereas the number of variables involved in determining the damage that natural catastrophes might cause is relatively limited, the effects of pandemics are more susceptible to human interventions—whether producing vaccines against a virus or enforcing quarantine measures of the sort that were belatedly put into place during the Ebola outbreak that spread in West Africa during the course of 2014.

How does Woo deal with this wall of uncertainties? The basic approach is the same as his modeling of events like earthquakes and hurricanes. His firm creates a very large set of randomly generated pandemics by synthesizing different assumptions about seven layers of risk. The first risk to consider is the probability of a pandemic occurring. There are more data to draw on than just the Spanish flu: between 1700 and 1900, for example, there were an estimated nine influenza pandemics. But there is no pattern that would allow for a sensible prediction of when the next pandemic is likely to come. So RMS also uses experts to estimate the frequencies at which there are jumps in viral characteristics that elude the defenses of humans' immune systems.

Having worked out the probabilities of a new virus strain emerging, the next step is the crucial one: working out what damage it would do. That calculation boils down to two parameters: infectiousness (that is, how fast a virus can spread) and virulence (that is, how many deaths does it cause in the infected population). The model categorizes possible pandemics by each of these characteristics, sorting each of them into one of seven buckets for infectiousness and six buckets for virulence. That means there are forty-two possible combinations of these parameters, some of which have never been observed before in real life.[6]

At the extremes you could assume 100 percent infectiousness and 100 percent mortality, a pandemic that wipes out everyone. Since that would presumably also take out reinsurers and investors, there isn't a lot of point to assuming that kind of pandemic. In practice, moreover, there is an inverse correlation between the two characteristics. The more virulent a virus, the greater the chance that it will kill its host before it can spread farther. Analysis suggests that the death rate for people infected during the Spanish flu was only around 2.5 percent.[7] The mortality rate for the 2014 Ebola outbreak was more like 60–70 percent.

The model now has a way of estimating how often new viruses are generated and of defining a range of characteristics that determine their potential to cause damage. The next step is to simulate the journey of a pandemic through the population in question (like catastrophe bonds, so-called excess-mortality bonds protect against risks in specific countries). That involves another set of calculations. One concerns the demographic profile of the population. How old you are matters for how often you come into contact with other people: young adults mix with many more people than the elderly do, which has an impact on how quickly viruses can spread. Age also has an impact on susceptibility to infection, although which age makes you vulnerable varies from pandemic to pandemic. Normally, the elderly are particularly at risk from the flu. In 1918, however, nearly half of the deaths occurred in young adults (primarily men) who were between twenty and forty years old. One suggestion, based on research into victims' tissue samples, is that the influenza strain involved in the Spanish flu triggered something called a "cytokine storm," a dangerous overreaction of the immune system that is more common among younger people.

RMS's model then makes a series of assumptions about where an outbreak begins: it matters to the spread of a virus whether it starts in a city or in the countryside. It also considers the capacity of authorities to respond to an outbreak. That means working through the various countermeasures that can be introduced to reduce the spread of disease: travel restrictions can be imposed, schools can be closed, and so on. It also means modeling the potential for vaccination programs in affected areas, although Woo currently assumes that a proper vaccine couldn't be developed within six months of an outbreak starting. That matters for the final set of estimations that the RMS model makes, on how quickly a pandemic might run through a population.

The model is now armed with an array of assumptions that can be combined to "create" a pandemic and simulate its path through a population. But creating one pandemic is not the idea: the game here is not one of prediction, but probability. So what the model does is randomly assign characteristics to create many thousands of different simulations. You might have one pandemic that is very virulent but whose spread can be curtailed by school closures, another that is highly infectious and starts in the most densely populated part of the country, another that kills everything in its path but burns itself out quickly. This process of randomized, repetitive modeling generates an "event set" of ten thousand pandemics, each one of which produces a grisly number: the deaths it would cause.

Woo's next job is to translate all the simulations that reside in the model into something that quantifies the probabilities of these losses occurring. The way he does so is to construct something called an "exceedance-probability curve." All of the ten thousand simulations are ranked according to the deaths they would cause and therefore what losses they would inflict. From these data,

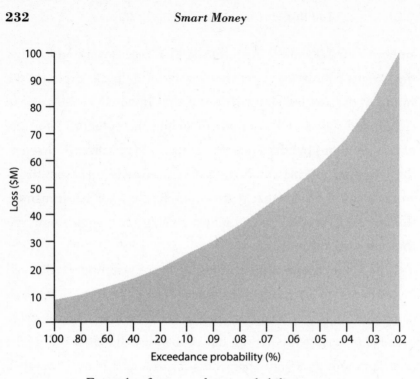

Example of an exceedance probability curve.

RMS can extract a curve that shows the full spectrum of possible pandemics, plotted to show their likelihood of taking place in any one year and the losses they would inflict. Figure 3 shows what a stylized exceedance-probability curve looks like.

The exceedance-probability curve is a way of extracting the bit of information that issuers and investors really need: the probability in any one year of specific numbers of extra deaths over expected mortality rates. Armed with that data, ratings agencies can assign a rating that is the macabre equivalent of a default probability on a corporate bond. The rating in turn helps set a framework for the pricing of the bond in the market.

LET'S NOW TURN TO Woo's assertion that his method for modeling the risk of catastrophe has lessons for other parts of finance. His approach is to dive into the structural causes of events and explicitly concentrate on the extreme risks. That was clearly not the way people thought about the American housing market prior to the crisis.

We saw in Chapter 2 how important AAA credit ratings were in reassuring investors in mortgage-backed securities that the risks were very low. In fact, as a judgment about the likelihood that these instruments would default, the AAA standard performed better than you might think. One surprising statistic to come out of the subprime crisis is from a little-reported analysis by Sun Young Park, now an assistant professor at the Korea Advanced Institute of Science and Technology. She analyzed the actual performance of subprime tranches of mortgage-backed securities—not collateralized-debt obligations, but the preceding step in the securitization chain—issued in the United States between 2004 and 2007 and looked at how many losses had actually been sustained. A total of $1.1 trillion in AAA-rated subprime MBS tranches were issued in that period, and Park identified a loss amount on these securities of $2.6 billion by August 2013. That amounts to a loss percentage of only 0.24 percent. At one level, the machinery of securitization worked.[8]

Don't worry: you did not imagine the financial crisis. The default rates on lower-rated tranches were way higher than they should have been: Park's analysis showed a loss percentage of 37 percent on AA-rated tranches, 56 percent on A-rated debt, and a whopping 69 percent on BBB-rated tranches. In relative terms, the ratings worked, but in terms of credit quality, these results were totally off-kilter. For comparison, according to Standard & Poor's, one of the rating agencies, the 2008 default rate on all US corporate bonds with "investment-grade" ratings of BBB and above was just 0.73 percent. The number of issues that were downgraded was also extraordinary: fewer than 20 percent of the tranches that were rated AAA at inception still had the same grade in February 2011.

All of which had the effect of panicking investors in these instruments—as well as those who were exposed to AAA-rated collateral via the repo markets and other channels. Even though the AAA rating is officially an assessment of default probabilities, recall that its greater significance is as a badge of safety. This was the same label that was plastered on the debt of countries such as the United States and Germany, after all. Although sovereigns can repay their obligations by increasing taxes and (for local-currency debt) printing money, that huge difference between countries and issuers of structured products was forgotten. In the minds of investors, a AAA rating meant simply that there was no need to worry; finding out that there was came as a huge shock. Even those fund managers who remained calm were often forced to sell downgraded holdings by mandates that required them to invest in assets only above a certain rating. So even though the securities were not defaulting in great numbers, huge losses still materialized because people were selling out when prices had dropped.

The gap between perception and reality for the top-rated tranches was still wide enough to cause huge damage, but it was not a chasm. Collateralized-debt obligations were a very different story. CDOs are instruments made up of the riskier slices of a lot of ordinary asset-backed securities. CDOs were supposed to benefit from diversification: mortgages pulled from different mortgage-backed securities were expected to perform differently, rather than undergo a synchronized swoon. That is why the senior tranches of CDOs were able to command AAA ratings when their raw materials were bits of mortgage-backed securities that had a lower rating. Abacus, a 2007 brew of subprime mortgages arranged by Goldman Sachs, was made up of 90 Baa2-rated mortgage-backed securities. A Baa2 rating is a Moody's rating and is equivalent to a BBB rating from Standard & Poor's: both sit at the bottom of what the credit-ratings agencies term investment-grade debt, several notches below the gold-plated AAA standard. Yet out of these lower ratings emerged a CDO that had a AAA rating on 79 percent of its contents.[9]

We now know that the modeling assumptions that led to this alchemy were wholly flawed. The ratings agencies reached their conclusions both by looking at historical default rates and by running models that calculated correlations between the different components of the CDOs—that is, the idea that if one went bad, the others would not. The particular model that became the industry standard for valuing CDOs—the Gaussian copula—was based on mathematical work that originally looked at survival rates of partners who have been bereaved. The date of death of a husband or wife is affected by when they are widowed, a phenomenon known as "broken-heart syndrome." A model that managed to capture the dependence between these two events and was used to price joint annuities in insurance was the inspiration for the model that calculated the probabilities that one set of mortgage defaults would be accompanied by another.

This is a world away from the way the agencies used to work. "We used to look at the worst possible losses in an impressionistic way," says a former employee of one of the three big agencies. "If unemployment went to Depression-era levels, we might assume that the default rate jumps to 4 percent and that there was a 50 percent decline in value of houses that banks foreclosed and sold. That's how we got to credit enhancement of 8 percent on AAA mortgages. It was not scientific. We were just trying to convey that triple AAA is as safe as the US government, and that BBB is like Mexico, not that AAA was a default probability of X percent."

This is the paradox of big data: an approach that tries to be more rigorous and data driven produces results that have a tendency to be taken on faith. "Part of what went wrong over the long term was two things: computing power and the Greenspan consensus [named for Alan Greenspan, a former chairman of the Federal Reserve] that markets worked," says the former employee. "The finance industry could slice, dice, and analyze information in ways they couldn't before. Information was available, which meant markets could function properly. People thought information asymmetry was the problem, and now that problem was solved. Everyone thought they could price risk. That was an illusion: you have to know what you are looking at."

What the agencies—and the industry as a whole—should have been looking at was the probability of a national downturn in American housing prices. Securitization is a technique that relies on diversification, which means that the thing it cannot survive is a systemic event that affects every asset in the pool. In the case of America's mortgage market, the catastrophic risk was a national housing crash. Real-estate crashes are a perennial cause of financial crises around the world. The history of the United States is a history of real-estate booms and busts: there is no secret about the tendency of house and land prices to fall after they have surged. The country's ability to build more and more housing is a pretty basic signal that prices ought not to get too out of hand: the entire population of the United States could fit in Texas with more than one acre per household.[10]

For various reasons—a lack of imagination, a surfeit of self-interest, the usefulness of simplifying assumptions and heuristics, and an unusually long period of calm in the national housing market—the models that underpinned the mortgage machine did not reach far enough back in time to consider the worst-case scenarios, let alone go beyond them; did not give enough weight to the risk of a systemic event that would render correlation modeling redundant because everything would start to move together; did not ask what would bring the edifice tumbling down. In short, they did not look closely enough at the extremes. "You cannot create a AAA out of single Bs," says a former head of structured finance at one of the ratings agencies. "In a single B recession, they all default."

Closer scrutiny of the tails was particularly important for a product like mortgage-backed securities, for two reasons. First, they are structured products. And second, they involve credit risk. Both introduce more danger. There is a distinction between corporate finance, which is about financing companies, and structured finance, which is about financing things like planes, ships, houses, and projects. When companies are financed, they can just issue debt and equity directly. When things get financed, a new entity needs to be created in order to issue debt and equity. This new firm pays back its investors with the cash flows that are associated with the asset in question: lease payments for an aircraft, for example, or mortgage payments on houses. This difference matters. A corporate-finance transaction can take advantage of an existing infrastructure of analysts and ratings agencies and a history of reporting and accounts. With structured finance, there is more legwork to be done. A company has to be created; analysis has to be done from scratch; investors have to be educated. That slows things down. But it also increases the risk of making assumptions that are wildly wrong.

Bad assumptions also matter more when it comes to "credit risk"—the risk that a borrower will default on their debt. Most other risks in finance are about movements: the direction and speed with which interest rates or exchange rates or stock markets go up or down. Credit risk is more about an event: a failure to pay. Credit risk is more likely to materialize quickly and to take people by surprise. The seller of a credit-default swap, which insures the buyer against the default of a particular borrower, is more likely to have obligations to pay up that can be triggered suddenly. If enough of these obligations are triggered at once, the provider of protection can be overwhelmed, a phenomenon known as "jump-to-default risk." There is a specific quality to credit that requires greater care.

All of which suggests that the type of catastrophe-risk modeling practiced by Woo does have something important to offer for assessing financial risks. That does not mean it should be fetishized: any model can be wrong. And financial risks present some very distinctive challenges. Whereas Woo is modeling events whose probabilities depend on exogenous factors—things that are external to the model itself—one of the major issues with financial markets is "endogeneity," changes that are generated within the system. The amount of money that goes into the cat-bond industry is not going to affect the chances of an earthquake occurring. By contrast, the amount of money that went into real estate had a causal impact on the probability and size of the crash that resulted. As we saw in the second chapter, just by going about its business, finance creates new risks.

An approach that is willing to delve deeply into the structural causes of risk and focus on the extreme scenarios is to be applauded, however. That is not exactly a new way of thinking for insurers, but it is one that is unusual in many parts of finance. Bankers and fund managers—and borrowers—are pretty dreadful at thinking about the worst when times are good. And regulators, too, are prone to being lulled into complacency by long periods of calm. Financial entrepreneurs have a lot of avenues to explore. The job of saving finance from itself is one of them.

Conclusion

Anyone who defends finance must recognize its inherent failings. There is a destructive logic to the way that the seething brains of finance innovate, experiment, standardize, and pursue opportunities. Even a financial industry populated by saints would have a tendency to excess, and this is a sector that is short of halos. The words that finance immediately conjures up—*bonuses, recklessness, greed, bastards, greedy bastards*—are absolutely part of the industry's narrative.

But this is also an industry that is home to creative minds grappling with gigantic problems. There are big banks, but there are also visionary entrepreneurs: finance is a playground for both. There are institutions skimming fat fees by sitting in the middle of transactions, and there are upstarts trying to connect buyers and sellers directly using the power of technology and big data. The 2007–2008 crisis is read by many as a warning against experimentation. But the false comfort of the familiar—rising property prices, high credit ratings, and so on—was what really landed us in this mess. Worse, it continues to seduce. A system that provides affluent households with mortgages is not what debt-laden Western societies need, yet it is the one we instinctively embrace.

This book has encountered all manner of problems to be solved. Too many of us die prematurely of cancer. Too few of us have sufficient savings for our retirements. The state needs to tie its spending more effectively to outcomes. More equity financing is needed in the worlds of property and student debt. Channeling credit to people who are on the periphery of the system is a more pressing problem in the wake of the subprime boom and bust in the United States.

As we have seen, financial innovators are grappling with each of these challenges—and many others. The creation of carbon markets as a mechanism for pricing carbon emissions is one example. Water scarcity is another huge, global issue. As an asset, water is neither clear nor liquid. There is no trading in water. There are subsidies galore. There is no global price. But demand is immense and rising. The growth in the world's population, expected to exceed 9 billion people by 2050, implies increased demand for freshwater, a finite resource, of about 64 billion cubic meters a year. Without a way of putting a value on water—and, in particular, on the use of water in agriculture—there is no obvious mechanism to ration consumption or increase efficiency in response to such thirst. Finance will find a way to compute that value.

My hope, by the end of this book, is that such a prospect sounds less disturbing than it may have at the start. When the figures come out on the proportion of graduates going into the financial services industry, the usual reaction is to assume that other industries simply must be more productive outlets for our brightest young people. But are other sectors really more useful? In his book *Finance and the Good Society*, Robert Shiller cites a statistic showing that

19.7 percent of America's labor force in 2002 was engaged in some form of guarding activity.[1] That doesn't scream social utility.

Financial innovation has made enormous contributions to society in the past, and it is primed to do so again. Indeed, the crisis of 2007–2008 has made it more likely that finance will be both creative and constructive. Financial entrepreneurs have the opportunity to rethink an industry that is more constrained, cautious, and cost conscious than before. They are also able to attract capital more easily: the amount of venture capital flowing into European financial-technology firms, for example, has not been this high since the dot-com era.

That is not to be complacent about finance. Growth and greed can distort good ideas. But when the next financial crisis comes, my bet is that it will stem from an established market, probably property, in which mainstream investors and profit-maximizing institutions have gotten carried away once again. The balance that regulators have to strike is watchfulness for the risks that can cause real economic damage and tolerance for the ideas that can produce real benefits. My belief is that tremendous good will come out of the financial industry in the coming years, thanks to the sorts of entrepreneurs and innovators we have met in the preceding pages. The next time someone says that finance is good for nothing but enriching bankers, think of them.

ACKNOWLEDGMENTS

This book was born from a special report on financial innovation that was published in the *Economist* in 2012, as well as from my reporting for the newspaper both before and since. I would like to thank John Micklethwait, the editor, for his initial decision to dispatch me into the world of the banks and all the colleagues I worked with in the subsequent years on the finance and economics section.

A special mention goes to Philip Coggan, who provided guidance, friendship, and bad jokes throughout. He and others were kind enough to read early drafts of the manuscript. My thanks go to Kevin Barrett, Richard Davies, James Dickson, and James Taylor for their comments. Not one of them said the draft was unimprovable, which was irritating. More annoying still, their comments did make it better. Damiano Brigo was also good enough to read through the chapter on catastrophe risk.

Many people within the industry spoke to me as part of the research for this book. It is in the nature of these things that some material was left on the cutting-room floor, but I am grateful to everyone who gave their time. As well as those mentioned in the book, special thanks go to Mark Wiedman and his colleagues at

BlackRock for the insights they shared on the world of exchange-traded funds and to Michael DuVally and his colleagues at Goldman Sachs for helping me to understand a new aircraft-financing instrument that the firm helped arrange.

Books are harder to write than articles, and I benefited enormously from the expertise and advice of Andrew Stuart, my agent; Lara Heimert, the publisher of Basic Books; and Roger Labrie, Collin Tracy, Leah Stecher, and Annette Wenda, each of whom improved the book immeasurably. At home, I took a finite resource—the patience of my gorgeous family—and used it all up. Julia, Eliza, Joe, and Kasia: thank you.

GLOSSARY

The financial industry can feel impenetrable, partly because of the amount of jargon it uses. I've tried to use everyday language throughout the book, but for nonfinance types the following is a quick guide to some of the terms that recur.

Adverse selection: The tendency for a product or market, particularly in the insurance sector, to attract higher-risk customers.

Basis risk: The risk that a **hedging** strategy will not work out because assets whose prices and risks are supposed to offset each other, with one rising as the other falls, do not behave as expected.

Bond: An IOU issued by a company or government, which entitles the lenders to get their initial money (or principal) back as well as income in the form of an interest payment. Because bonds offer investors a fixed return, they are known as fixed-income assets. Like loans, bonds are a form of debt. Unlike loans, they are highly tradable and their ownership is very dispersed.

Clearinghouse: A clearinghouse stands in between buyers and sellers in financial transactions and is designed to reduce counterparty risk. When an uncleared derivatives contract moves onto a clearinghouse, it divides into two: a contract between the buyer and the clearinghouse and a matching contract between the seller and the clearinghouse.

Collateral: The security that borrowers put up to protect their creditors in the event of default. The collateral on a mortgage is the property on which the mortgage is written. Lending that does not have any collateral associated with it is called unsecured lending and will carry a higher interest rate. In **derivatives** transactions, more collateral (or "margin") can be demanded as the values of specific contracts go up and down.

Collateralized-debt obligations: The next step in the **securitization** process after the creation of asset-backed securities is the CDO. CDOs are instruments made up of the riskier slices of a lot of ordinary asset-backed securities. They are then sliced into different tranches: the most senior tranches of CDOs of mortgage-backed securities were given high ratings during the most recent US housing boom because the performance of all the different mortgages in the pool was thought to be diversified.

Counterparty risk: The risk that the other party to a contract will not live up to its obligations. The counterparty risk in an interest-rate swap is that one of the parties to the swap will not pay up.

Credit-default swap: A credit-default swap is a form of insurance against default by a bond issuer.

Credit ratings: An evaluation by a credit-rating agency of the creditworthiness of a debtor. Ratings are widely used by investors and are embedded in international rules, including those on how much equity banks have to use to fund themselves.

Derivatives: A financial instrument that derives its value from another underlying asset or entity.

Equity: The riskiest slice of the capital structure, equity is the owners' interest in an asset. An equity investment entitles its holders to whatever is left over after debts have been paid off. Equity also absorbs any losses first.

Futures: A contract to buy or sell an asset at a specified future date for a specified price. Futures contracts are traded on exchanges; forwards, which do the same thing as futures, are private, "over-the-counter" agreements.

Hedging: An investment strategy designed to offset price movements in one asset by holding a position in another. A farmer might lock in a price for his crop via the futures market, hedging himself against a sharp fall in market prices.

High-frequency trading: A trading strategy that is characterized by extreme speed. High-frequency traders pursue a variety of investment approaches, from following short-term price trends to making markets.

Information asymmetry: When one party knows more about a transaction than the other. Companies with very short track records or people seeking health-insurance coverage will, for example, usually be better informed about their circumstances than a potential equity investor or an insurance provider.

Leverage: The amount of debt that a borrower carries relative to equity. If a bank has 5 percent equity, it has a leverage ratio of twenty to one. Leverage magnifies the effects of upward or downward price movements. The term is also used when investors gain greater exposure to price movements by buying derivatives than they would do by simply buying the underlying asset.

Liquidity: The capacity to buy and sell assets easily. Liquid assets, like equities and government bonds, are easily traded. Illiquid ones, like property, are not.

Maturity transformation: The process by which a bank borrows for shorter durations than it loans money out. An example of maturity transformation is when deposits, which can be taken out instantly, are used to fund mortgages, which can last for decades.

Options: A contract that gives the owner the right, but not the obligation, to buy or sell an asset at an agreed price. A call option confers the right to buy, and a put option confers the right to sell.

Private equity: An asset class in which fund managers typically take large stakes in unlisted companies with the aim of selling out at a profit after a number of years. Private-equity firms have widened their activities in recent years and now participate in other areas, such as asset management, lending, and hedge funds.

Repurchase (repo) agreement: A form of short-term lending in which a borrower sells securities and agrees to buy them back at a later date at a slightly higher price. The securities act as collateral in the event of a default by the borrower.

Securitization: The process of bundling together a lot of different income-generating assets into a single bond, or security. Residential mortgage-backed securities take the mortgage payments made by a lot of different home owners, for example, and funnel them to investors. Other assets that are securitized include credit-card receivables, car loans, corporate loans, music royalties, and tobacco-settlement fees. These asset-backed securities are then sliced up, or tranched, so that they have a capital structure with equity investors at the bottom and debt investors at the top.

Venture capital: A form of equity investment in early-stage companies.

NOTES

NOTES TO PREFACE

1. "Translational Research: 4 Ways to Fix the Clinical Trial," *Nature* 477 (2011): 526–528, http://www.nature.com/news/2011/110928 /full/477526a.html.

2. "WaMu Is Seized, Sold Off to J. P. Morgan, in Largest Failure in US Banking History," *Wall Street Journal*, September 26, 2008.

3. Volcker's remarks were made at a 2009 conference ("Paul Volcker: Think More Boldly," *Wall Street Journal*, December 14, 2009). Krugman's columns in the *New York Times* have frequently questioned the utility of financial innovation; see, for example, "Destructive Creativity," January 18, 2010.

4. "The Great Career Debate: Google Versus Goldman," October 31, 2013, http://www.inc.com/kimberly-weisul/the-great-career-debate -google-versus-goldman.html.

NOTES TO CHAPTER 1

1. For more on the history of money, a plug here for *Paper Promises: Money, Debt and the New World Order* (London: Allen Lane, 2011), by my colleague Philip Coggan.

2. Vincent Bignon, "Cigarette Money and Black-Market Prices During the 1948 German Miracle" (EconomiX Working Papers from University of Paris West–Nanterre la Défense, 2009).

3. For a retelling of the history of credit and money, see David Graeber's *Debt: The First 5,000 Years* (Brooklyn: Melville House, 2011).

4. K. V. Nagarajan, "The Code of Hammurabi: An Economic Interpretation," *International Journal of Business and Social Science* (May 2011).

5. See, for example, Hal Hershfield et al., "Increasing Saving Behaviour Through Age-Progressed Renderings of the Future Self," *Journal of Marketing Research* (2011).

6. Ron Harris, "The Institutional Dynamics of Early Modern Eurasian Trade: The *Commenda* and the Corporation," *Journal of Economic Behavior and Organization* 71, no. 3 (2009).

7. Eric Lonergan writes extremely well about this in his book *Money* (Durham, England: Acumen, 2009).

8. Marine insurance was still setting the terms at the start of the twentieth century: the first car insured at Lloyd's of London in 1901 was covered by a marine policy on the basis that it was a ship navigating on dry land.

9. Eric Briys and Didier Joos de ter Beest, "The Zaccaria Deal: Contract and Options to Fund a Genoese Shipment of Alum to Bruges in 1298" (paper presented at the XIV International Economic History Congress, Helsinki, August 2006).

10. For a full history of the Amsterdam Stock Exchange, see Lodewijk Petram, *The World's First Stock Exchange* (New York: Columbia University Press, 2014).

11. Jennifer Anne Carlson, "The Economics of Fire Protection: From the Great Fire of London to Rural/Metro," *Institute of Economic Affairs* (April 2005).

12. William Goetzmann, "Fibonacci and the Financial Revolution" (NBER Working Paper 10352, March 2004).

13. Chris Lewin, "The Creation of Actuarial Science," *Zentralblatt für Didaktik der Mathematik* 33, no. 2 (2001): 61–66.

14. François Velde and David Weir, "The Financial Market and Government Debt Policy in France, 1746–1793," *Journal of Economic History* (March 1992).

15. For more on the role of technology in propelling financial innovation, see Stelios Michalopoulos, Luc Laeven, and Ross Levine, "Financial Innovation and Endogenous Growth" (NBER Working Paper 51356, September 2009).

16. Richard Sylla, "A Historical Primer on the Business of Credit Ratings" (paper prepared for a conference of the World Bank, Washington, DC, March 2001).

17. Andrew Odlyzko, "Collective Hallucinations and Inefficient Markets: The British Railway Mania of the 1840s," *SSRN Electronic Journal* (2010).

18. Peter Tufano, "Business Failure, Judicial Intervention and Financial Innovation: Restructuring US Railroads in the Nineteenth Century," *Business History Review* (1997).

19. Robert Shiller, "The Invention of Inflation-Indexed Bonds in America" (NBER Working Paper 10183, December 2003). For a more comprehensive history, see Franklin Allen and Douglas Gale, *Financial Innovation and Risk Sharing* (Cambridge, MA: MIT Press, 1994).

20. Sometimes, they are more important. As policy makers try to find a way to avoid bailing out banks in a future financial crisis, one answer is a new security issued by banks called "contingent convertible" bonds, or CoCos for short. The idea behind CoCos is that bondholders are forcibly converted into shareholders when a bank's level of capital falls below a certain threshold, so that when a financial institution gets into trouble, its equity cushion is automatically plumped up. Financial engineering is one answer to a crisis partly caused by financial engineering.

21. Saumitra Jha, "Sharing the Future: Financial Innovation and Innovators in Solving the Political Economy Challenges of Development" (Stanford Graduate School of Business Research Paper 2093, 2011).

22. Alan Morrison and William Wilhelm Jr., *Investment Banking: Institutions, Politics and Law* (Oxford: Oxford University Press, 2007).

23. Richard Green and Susan Wachter, "The American Mortgage in Historical and International Context," *Journal of Economic Perspectives* (2005).

24. The story of the first interest-rate futures and many other derivatives is told by Richard Sandor in his book *Good Derivatives* (Hoboken, NJ: John Wiley & Sons, 2012). The history of credit-default swaps is recounted in Gillian Tett, *Fool's Gold: How Unrestrained Greed Corrupted a Dream, Shattered Global Markets and Unleashed a Catastrophe* (London: Abacus, 2009). Data on the growth of the derivatives are

available from "The Global Derivatives Market: An Introduction" (white paper, Deutsche Börse Group, 2008).

25. The full story behind the Black-Scholes equation is well told in George Szpiro, *Pricing the Future: Finance, Physics and the 300-Year Journey to the Black-Scholes Equation* (New York: Basic Books, 2011). The calculations about Thales can be found in Vasiliki Makropoulou and Raphael Markellos, "What Is the Fair Rent Thales Should Have Paid?" (presented at the proceedings of the Seventh Hellenic-European Conference on Computer Mathematics and Its Applications, 2005).

26. Morrison and Wilhelm, *Investment Banking*.

27. Earl Thompson, "The Tulipmania: Fact or Artifact?," *Public Choice* 130, nos. 1–2 (2007).

28. S. H. Haber, "Industrial Concentration and the Capital Markets: A Comparative Study of Brazil, Mexico and the United States," *Journal of Economic History* (1991); Luigi Guiso, Paola Sapienza, and Luigi Zingales, "Does Local Financial Development Matter?" (NBER Working Paper 8923, May 2002); Thorsten Beck, Asli Demirguc-Kunt, and Ross Levine, "Finance, Inequality and Poverty: Cross-Country Evidence" (NBER Working Paper 10979, December 2004); Kathleen Beegle, Rajeev Dehejia, and Roberta Gatti, "Child Labour, Crop Shocks and Credit Constraints" (NBER Working Paper 10088, November 2003).

Notes to Chapter 2

1. Also unkindly known as *This Spreadsheet Is Different*, following the 2013 revelation of an Excel error in Reinhart and Rogoff's analysis of the relationship between public debt and growth. That mistake should not detract from the excellent empirical analysis they do in the book, which was published by Princeton University Press in 2009.

2. Tenney Frank, "The Financial Crisis of 33 AD," *American Journal of Philology* 56, no. 4 (1935).

3. Oscar Gelderblom and Joost Jonker, "Completing a Financial Revolution: The Finance of the Dutch East India Trade and the Rise of the Amsterdam Capital Market, 1595–1612," *Journal of Economic History* (2004).

4. Peter Tufano, "Financial Innovation and First-Mover Advantages," *Journal of Financial Economics* (1989); Peter Tufano, "Financial Innovation," *Handbook of the Economics of Finance* (2003).

5. "The Dojima Rice Market and the Origins of Futures Trading" (Harvard Business School Case Study, November 2010).

6. Minos Zombanakis, "The Life and Good Times of Libor," *Financial World* (June 2012).

7. Nicola Gennaioli, Andrei Shleifer, and Robert Vishny, "Neglected Risks, Financial Innovation and Financial Fragility," *Journal of Financial Economics* (2012).

8. "Financial Globalisation: Retreat or Reset?" (McKinsey Global Institute, February 2013).

9. Marcin Kasperczyk and Philipp Schnabl, "How Safe Are Money Market Funds?," *Quarterly Journal of Economics* 128 (2013).

10. Nicola Lacetera, Devin Pope, and Justin Sydnor, "Heuristic Thinking and Limited Attention in the Car Market" (NBER Working Paper 17030, June 2011).

11. The intuitive answer is $0.10, but that yields a total of $1.20. The correct answer is that the ball costs $0.05. No matter how many times I see this question, I cannot stop the wrong answer from immediately occurring to me. Financial traders outperformed in a test administered by Volker Thoma of the University of East London, presented at the University's Research and Knowledge Exchange Conference in June 2013. Daniel Kahneman's work is distilled in his own *Thinking Fast and Slow* (New York: Farrar, Straus, and Giroux, 2011).

12. Benjamin Keys et al., "Did Securitisation Lead to Lax Screening? Evidence from Subprime Loans," *Quarterly Journal of Economics* 125 (2010).

13. Manuel Adelino, "How Much Do Investors Rely on Ratings? The Case of Mortgage-Backed Securities" (2009), http://ssrn.com /abstract=1425216.

14. Financial Crisis Inquiry Commission, *The Financial Crisis Inquiry Commission Report, Authorized Edition* (New York: PublicAffairs, 2011), 260.

15. Jeffrey G. MacIntosh, "High Frequency Traders: Angels or Devils?" (Commentary no. 391, CD Howe Institute, October 2013).

16. "Microwave Arms Race Gathers Pace," *Futures and Options World*, August 27, 2013.

17. "Findings Regarding the Market Events of May 6, 2010" (Report of the Staffs of the CFTC and SEC to the Joint Advisory Committee on Emerging Regulatory Issues, September 30, 2010).

18. High-frequency trading is used in a number of strategies, of which market making is just one. Some high-frequency traders are momentum traders, riding the wave of a particular trend in securities pricing. Others arbitrage price differences.

19. See note 17 above.

20. "High Frequency Trading: Measurement, Detection and Response" (Credit Suisse, December 2012).

21. Michael Lewis, *Flash Boys: Cracking the Money Code* (London: Allen Lane, 2014).

22. "The Kay Review of UK Equity Markets and Long-Term Decision Making" (House of Commons Business, Innovation and Skills Committee, July 25, 2013).

23. Statement of George U. Sauter, the Vanguard Group (Securities and Exchange Commission, Market Structure Roundtable, June 2010).

24. Josh Lerner and Peter Tufano, "The Consequences of Financial Innovation: A Counterfactual Research Agenda" (NBER Working Paper 16780, February 2011).

25. The firm's colorful story is told in a 1999 book called *The Predictors* (New York: Owl Books), by Thomas Bass.

26. Rachel Adams, "Goldman Explores Sale of Market-Making Unit," *New York Times*, April 1, 2014.

27. It is not the best quote of the crisis, however. That honor goes to President George W. Bush, reassuring the world's finance ministers in November 2008 that Hank Paulson, his treasury secretary, was on top of things: "You folks don't need to worry. Hank's got a handle on this. He's going to freeze that liquidity."

28. Elizabeth Ledrut and Christian Upper, "The US Paper Crunch, 1967–70," *BIS Quarterly Review* (December 2007).

Notes to Chapter 3

1. "British Homes Gain £57 Billion in Value During 2012," *Zoopla*, January 11, 2013; "Bricks and Slaughter," *Economist*, March 3, 2011.

2. National Association of Realtors (August 2014), http://www.realtor.org/research-and-statistics.

3. We will ignore transactions costs, interest payments, redemption fees, and the like for the sake of simplicity.

4. Meghan Busse et al., "Projection Bias in the Car and Housing Markets" (NBER Working Paper 18212, July 2012).

5. Hugo Benitez-Silva et al., "How Well Do Individuals Predict the Selling Prices of Their Homes?" (Levy Economics Institute Working Paper 571, 2008).

6. Figures come from Nationwide's house-price index.

7. Neil Monnery, *Safe as Houses? A Historical Analysis of Property Prices* (London: London Publishing Partnership, 2011).

8. Edward Glaeser, "A Nation of Gamblers: Real-Estate Speculation and American History" (NBER Working Paper 18825, February 2013).

9. The leverage-ratio requirement may vary from jurisdiction to jurisdiction.

10. Thomas Hoenig, "Back to Basics: A Better Alternative to Basel Capital Rules" (speech at the Federal Deposit Insurance Corporation, Washington, DC, September 14, 2012).

11. Stephen G. Cecchetti and Enisse Kharroubi, "Why Does Financial Sector Growth Crowd Out Real Economic Growth?" (Bank for International Settlements, September 2013).

12. Monnery, *Safe as Houses?*

Notes to Chapter 4

1. Sir Ronald stepped down as chairman at the start of 2014, but continues to pursue the social-investment agenda via a Group of 8 initiative.

2. Stephen King, *When the Money Runs Out* (New Haven, CT: Yale University Press, 2013).

3. "Entitlements in America," *Economist,* May 25, 2013.

4. Jon Baron and Isabel Sawhill, "We Need a New Start for Head Start" (Brookings Institution, March 2010).

5. "Test, Learn, Adapt: Developing Public Policy with Randomised Controlled Trials" (United Kingdom Cabinet Office Behavioural Insights Team, 2012).

6. William Foster and Gail Fine, "How Nonprofits Get Really Big," *Stanford Social Innovation Review* (Spring 2007), http://www.ssireview.org/articles/entry/how_nonprofits_get_really_big.

7. John List, "The Market for Charitable Giving," *Journal of Economic Perspectives* (Spring 2011).

8. Dan Ariely, Anat Bracha, and Stephan Meier, "Doing Well or Doing Good? Image Motivation and Monetary Incentives in Behaving Prosocially" (Federal Reserve Bank of Boston, August 2007).

NOTES TO CHAPTER 5

1. Jack Scannell et al., "Diagnosing the Decline in Pharmaceutical Efficiency," *Nature Reviews Drug Discovery* 11 (March 2012); Frank Lichtenberg, "Pharmaceutical Innovation and Longevity Growth in 30 Developing and High-Income Countries, 2000–09" (NBER Working Paper 18235, July 2012). The research was supported by Pfizer.

2. David Fagnan et al., "Can Financial Engineering Cure Cancer?," *American Economic Review: Papers and Proceedings* (2013).

3. Andrew Lo, "Fear, Greed and Financial Crises: A Cognitive Neurosciences Perspective," in *Handbook of Systemic Risk,* edited by Jean-Pierre Fouque and Joseph Langsam (Cambridge: Cambridge University Press, 2013).

4. John Coates, *The Hour Between Dog and Wolf* (London: Fourth Estate, 2012).

5. Securities Industry and Financial Markets Association, US Bond Market Issuance and Outstanding, September 2014, and US Equity Statistics, July 2014, http://www.SIFMA.org.

6. There is also the not-so-small matter of the tax deductibility of debt, a distortion so big that everyone knows it is a problem and no one has the faintest idea how to remove it.

7. The full story behind the Black-Scholes equation is very well told in George Szpiro, *Pricing the Future: Finance, Physics and the 300-Year Journey to the Black-Scholes Equation* (New York: Basic Books, 2011).

8. "Entitlements in America," *Economist*, May 25, 2013.

9. "The Financial Impact of Longevity Risk" (International Monetary Fund, April 2012).

10. "World Population Prospects: The 2012 Revision" (United Nations, 2013).

11. "The Pensions Outlook, 2012" (OECD, 2012).

12. "The Retirement Savings Crisis? Is It Worse than We Think?" (National Institute on Retirement Security, June 2013).

13. "The 2013 Retirement Confidence Survey: Perceived Savings Needs Outpace Reality for Many" (Employee Benefit Research Institute, March 2013); Annamaria Lusardi, "Planning and Saving for Retirement" (working paper, Dartmouth College, December 2003).

14. Daniel Read, George Loewenstein, and Shobana Kalyanaraman, "Mixing Virtue and Vice," *Journal of Behavioral Decision Making* (1999).

15. Annamaria Lusardi and Olivia Mitchell, "Financial Literacy and Planning: Implications for Retirement Wellbeing" (NBER Working Paper 17078, May 2011).

16. John Beshears et al., "The Impact of Employer Matching on Savings Plan Participation Under Automatic Enrolment" (NBER Working Paper 13352, August 2007).

17. Anne Tergesen, "401(k) Law Suppresses Saving for Retirement," *Wall Street Journal*, July 7, 2011.

18. M. Keith Chen, Venkat Lakshminarayanan, and Laurie Santos, "How Basic Are Behavioural Biases? Evidence from Capuchin Monkey Trading Behaviour," *Journal of Political Economy* (2006).

19. Shlomo Bernartzi and Richard Thaler, "Behavioural Economics and the Retirement Savings Crisis," *Science* (March 8, 2013).

20. James Choi et al., "Small Cues Change Savings Choices" (NBER Working Paper 17843, February 2012).

21. Amos Tversky and Daniel Kahnemann, "Judgment Under Uncertainty: Heuristics and Biases," *Science* (September 1974).

22. "Reverse Mortgages: Report to Congress" (Consumer Financial Protection Bureau, June 2012).

23. Esteban Calvo, Kelly Haverstick, and Natalia Zhivan, "Determinants and Consequences of Moving Decisions for Older Americans" (Center for Retirement Research at Boston College, August 2009).

24. "Reverse Mortgages: Report to Congress" (Consumer Financial Protection Bureau, June 2012).

25. Geoffrey Wilson Clark, *Betting on Lives: The Culture of Life Insurance in England, 1695–1775* (Manchester: Manchester University Press, 1999).

Notes to Chapter 6

1. John Haltiwanger, Ron Jarmin, and Javier Miranda, "Who Creates Jobs? Small vs. Large vs. Young" (NBER Working Paper 16300, August 2010).

2. Martin Schmalz, David Sraer, and David Thesmar, "Housing Collateral and Entrepreneurship" (NBER Working Paper 19680, 2013); Manuel Adelino, Antoinette Schoar, and Felipe Severino, "House Prices, Collateral and Self-Employment" (NBER Working Paper 18868, 2013).

3. Stephen Kaplan and John Lerner, "It Ain't Broke: The Past, Present and Future of Venture Capital," *Journal of Applied Corporate Finance* 22 (2010); "We Have Met the Enemy and He Is Us: Lessons from Twenty Years of the Kauffman Foundation's Investments in Venture Capital Funds and the Triumph of Hope over Experience" (Kauffman Foundation, May 2012).

4. The firm was initially called Maritime and Auto Security Solutions, but was renamed in 2014.

5. Felix Salmon, "The Idiocy of Crowds," September 23, 2013, Reuters.com.

6. James Montier, *The Little Book of Behavioural Investing* (Hoboken, NJ: John Wiley & Sons, 2010).

7. Gustaf Torngren and Henry Montgomery, "Worse than Chance? Performance and Confidence Among Professionals and Laypeople in the Stock Market," *Journal of Behavioural Finance* 5 (2004).

8. Hedge funds now like to claim that they are there to hedge investors in the bad times and that they should be judged on the years like 2008, when they performed well in relative terms. Having spent the

precrisis years boasting about their ability to generate absolute returns, this sounds like post hoc positioning.

9. "We Have Met the Enemy and He Is Us."

10. Ajay Agrawal, Christian Catalini, and Avi Goldfarb, "Some Simple Economics of Crowdfunding" (NBER Working Paper 19133, June 2013).

11. Miguel Palacios Lleras, *Investing in Human Capital* (Cambridge: Cambridge University Press 2004).

12. Gillian Tett, *Fool's Gold: How Unrestrained Greed Corrupted a Dream, Shattered Global Markets and Unleashed a Catastrophe* (London: Abacus, 2009).

13. Donghoon Lee, "Household Debt and Credit: Student Debt" (Federal Reserve Bank of New York, 2013); "Degrees of Debt," *Economist*, July 6, 2013; "Not What It Used to Be," *Economist*, December 1, 2012.

14. "Young Student Loan Borrowers Retreat from Housing and Auto Markets," Liberty Street Economics blog (Federal Reserve Bank of New York, April 2013).

15. Jeffrey Brown, Chichun Fang, and Francisco Gomes, "Risks and Returns to Education" (NBER Working Paper 18300, 2012).

16. Stephen Teng Sum and Constantine Yannelis, "Credit Constraints and Higher Education: Evidence from Financial Deregulation" (University Library of Munich MPRA Paper 48726, 2013).

17. Philippe Belley and Lance Lochner, "The Changing Role of Family Income and Ability in Determining Educational Achievement" (NBER Working Paper 13527, 2007); Claire Callender and Jon Jackson, "Fear of Debt and Higher Education Participation" (Families and Social Capital ESRC Research Group, 2004).

18. Deborah Gage, "The Venture Capital Secret: 3 Out of 4 Start-Ups Fail," *Wall Street Journal*, September 20, 2012.

NOTES TO CHAPTER 7

1. "Back to Basics: A Better Alternative to Basel Capital Rules" (speech by Thomas Hoenig of the Federal Deposit Insurance Corporation to the American Banker Regulatory Symposium, September 12, 2012). The Royal Bank of Scotland figure comes from the Financial Services

Authority's official report "The Failure of the Royal Bank of Scotland" (December 2011).

2. Nesta, "Banking on Each Other," April 25, 2013, http://www .nesta.org.uk/publications/banking-each-other-rise-peer-peer-lending -businesses.

3. "Withering Away," *Economist,* May 19, 2012.

4. Harry DeAngelo and René Stulz, "Why High Leverage Is Optimal for Banks" (NBER Working Paper 19139, August 2013).

NOTES TO CHAPTER 8

1. Victor Stango, "Are Payday Lending Markets Competitive?" *Regulation* (Fall 2012); "National Survey of Unbanked and Underbanked Households" (Federal Deposit Insurance Corporation, 2011).

2. "Margin Calls," *Economist,* February 16, 2013.

3. Meta Brown et al., "The Financial Crisis at the Kitchen Table: Trends in Household Debt and Credit," *Current Issues in Economics and Finance* 19 (2013).

4. Atif Mian and Amir Sufi, "The Consequences of Mortgage Credit Expansion: Evidence from the 2007 Mortgage Default Crisis" (NBER Working Paper 13936, April 2008).

5. Brown et al., "Financial Crisis at the Kitchen Table."

6. For a provocative critique of this evolution, try Amar Bhidé, *A Call for Judgment* (Oxford: Oxford University Press, 2010).

7. Alberto Alesina, Francesca Lotti, and Paolo Emilio Mistrulli, "Do Women Pay More for Credit? Evidence from Italy" (NBER Working Paper 14202, July 2008).

8. http://houseofdebt.org/2014/04/07/the-financial-vulnerability-of -americans.html.

9. Theresa Kuchler, "Sticking to Your Plan: Hyperbolic Discounting and Credit-Card Debt Paydown" (Stanford University, January 2013).

10. Melissa Schettini Kearney et al., "Making Savers Winners: An Overview of Prize-Linked Savings Products" (NBER Working Paper 16433, October 2010); Melissa Schettini Kearney, "State Lotteries and Consumer Behaviour" (NBER Working Paper 9330, November 2002).

11. Robert Shiller, *The New Financial Order* (Princeton, NJ: Princeton University Press, 2003).

12. Anne Murphy, "Lotteries in the 1690s: Investment or Gamble?," *Financial History Review* (October 2005).

NOTES TO CHAPTER 9

1. Giuseppe Longo, "The Tunguska Event," in *Comet/Asteroid Impacts and Human Society: An Interdisciplinary Approach,* edited by Peter Bobrowsky and Hans Rickman (Berlin: Springer, 2007).

2. To be precise, a special-purpose vehicle set up by the sponsoring insurer is the issuer of the bond. That protects investors from having their money locked up in a bankruptcy process if the issuer goes bust.

3. Goetz von Peter, Sebastian von Dahlen, and Sweta Saxena, "Unmitigated Disasters? New Evidence on the Macroeconomic Costs of Natural Catastrophes" (BIS Working Paper 394, December 2012). A charitable cat bond is one potential answer to this problem of uninsured countries. People would donate ahead of a disaster, and the cash would be released in the event of catastrophe striking.

4. Howard Kunreuther and Erwann Michel-Kerjan, *At War with the Weather* (Cambridge, MA: MIT Press, 2009).

5. "Lake Monsters," *Economist,* November 3, 2012.

6. K. D. Patterson, *Pandemic Influenza, 1700–1900: A Study in Historical Epidemiology* (Lanham, MD: Rowan & Littlefield, 1986).

7. Jeffrey Taubenberger and David Morens, "1918 Influenza: The Mother of All Pandemics," *Emerging Infectious Diseases* (January 2006).

8. Sun Young Park, "The Size of the Subprime Shock" (unpublished, 2011). Figures from 2013 supplied directly to the author.

9. Abacus is famous principally for being a transaction that landed Goldman in trouble with the Securities and Exchange Commission. The supersenior tranche in Abacus was not rated, but since AAA is as high as the rating scale goes, it too would have received this rating.

10. Edward Glaeser, "A Nation of Gamblers: Real-Estate Speculation and American History" (NBER Working Paper 18825, February 2013).

NOTES TO CONCLUSION

1. Robert Shiller, *Finance and the Good Society* (Princeton, NJ: Princeton University Press, 2012).

INDEX

AAA credit ratings, 49–51,
233–236

AARP Public Policy Institute,
report on home ownership
by, 139

Abacus, 235

Accenture, 54, 56

Adaptive-market hypothesis,
115–116

Adelino, Manuel, 49

Adoption, SIB program for, 97

Adverse selection, 21, 174, 175,
182

AIG (American International
Group), 65

AIR Worldwide, 222, 225

Alabama, land boom in, 74–75

Algorithms, 53–54, 56–57, 62–63,
113, 202, 216–217

Alibaba.com, 219

Allia, 108

Alzheimer's disease, megafund for,
122

Amazon, 162, 216–217, 219

American Diabetes Association,
102

American Dream Downpayment
Act of 2003, 78

American International Group
(AIG), 65

American Railroad Journal, 24

American Research and
Development Corporation,
150

Amsterdam Stock Exchange,
14–15, 24, 38

Anchoring effect, 137–138

Annuities, 20–22, 139

Apax Partners, 91

Aristotle, 10

Asian debt crisis (1990s), x, 30

Asian Development Bank, 27

Auto-enrollment in pension
schemes, 135

Auto-escalation, 135–136

Availability heuristic, 73

Baby boomers, retirement rate of,
125

Bailouts, xi, 35, 65

Bank, derivation of word, 12

Bank deregulation, effect of on
college enrollments, 171

Bank for International
Settlements (BIS), 224, 226

Bank of America, 98